Dailiness

MARK JARMAN

Dailiness

ESSAYS ON POETRY

PAUL DRY BOOKS

Philadelphia 2020

First Paul Dry Books edition, 2020

Paul Dry Books, Inc.
Philadelphia, Pennsylvania
www.pauldrybooks.com

Printed in the United States of America

Library of Congress Control Number: 2019955147

ISBN-13: 978-1-58988-141-9

For Amy

Cause me to hear thy lovingkindness
in the morning . . .

Contents

Preface

THE POETRY OF DAILY LIFE

A poet friend of mine once asked me not long after she had married for the first time what I thought was the secret of married life. I said there was no secret. Then I said that I thought it was daily life. Two people make a daily life together which they can enjoy. They may have children (my wife and I do); they may have pets (we have two cats); they may have professions which absorb and occupy them (we do); they may have all sorts of ways of being a family, a part of society, a culture, a nation, a world, a universe, the mind of God, but they are together daily, because they want to be. Even if separated by spans of time and distance, they are aware of each other and need to be aware of each other every day. They have some way of enjoying their mornings, afternoons, evenings, and nights together. When I thought of this response to my friend's question, since I had been married nearly forty years and she had been married less than one, I realized that the answer was in no way self-evident. It was an answer which, for me, had arisen from decades of marriage to one person, daily life through forty years with one person. Still, as far as I could see, life together was daily life. It was not a secret, except if it could be thought of as an open secret. The terms quotidian and mundane may have drab connotations, but the diurnal and the solar have cosmic resonance. The joy of these sequences of time may be what we call life. It may be called everyday, even commonplace, but without the foundation of time, there is no ground for living. In times of trial, to want one's life back is to desire to return to daily life, its ordinariness, its dailiness, especially when it is shared with someone else.

Poetry for me is deeply involved in this definition. Not only poets but all artists work in some daily routine, from the singer (my wife is a singer) who must practice every day to the poet like me who spends a part of every day looking at drafts and nudging them toward completion, and if lucky starting a new poem and even luckier finishing a poem. Dailiness like life itself is a serious joy if it is free of stress, pain, tragedy. No matter how you may be separated from your art or your life, your desire is to return to it one day.

Daily life is the native country where we feel at home, wherever it may be, however it may manifest itself. A return to dailiness after any period away may be a thing to long for, as an essential part of oneself. Otherwise, the only pleasure in exile is the hope that it will end. I do not believe alienation or estrangement is desirable. I do believe that the dying, too, would prefer to pull back from their suffering and return to living, going on, rather than coming to their end.

The scene in Thornton Wilder's *Our Town* in which the character Emily, deceased, is able to return to life for a single day has influenced my thinking. But I also have in mind a poem by Wallace Stevens, "Large Red Man Reading." The poem imagines the dead, "ghosts," returning to earth just to hear a living person read to them.

There were those that returned to hear him read from the
    poem of life,

> Of the pans above the stove, the pots on the table, the tulips
>   among them.
> They were those that would have wept to step barefoot into
>   reality . . .

I am trying to avoid bromides and platitudes and to speak from my own experience of desiring at all times, especially in extremity, simply a return to a daily sense of things. The importance of daily life as the location of my work as a poet is something I can't deny and the poetry that matters to me, like the poetry read from Stevens's "poem of life," affirms the reality of life's dailiness.

When my father died, on his eighty-ninth birthday, his children and most of his grandchildren were present. When I looked at him, I recognized that he had left both his body and time. Time was no longer relevant to him. To his survivors, yes, time was crucial, but the eternity that he had entered made time obsolete. Beforehand, he was on the outskirts of eternity. Now time, like daily life, had stopped. There were no more days to write his sermons (he was a Protestant minister) or finish his paintings (a hobby he had taken up seriously in retirement). In my last telephone conversation with him, two weeks before he died, he was euphoric from the effect of his medications, but also because he could imagine living with this disease (he had pancreatic cancer) for the rest of his life. He believed he had plenty of time, a condition he could live with, and a succession of days ahead for what he liked to do. It gave us both pleasure to think of that, for him to say he would live with this until he died.

To live with something is to get used to it over a span of days. My father was already refusing food a week before he died, worrying his wife, my stepmother, making those of his children who lived a distance from him want to get to him. When my middle sister reached him a few days before I did, she dealt with his last expenditure of energy, wrestling him to stay in his bed while he raved comically, "I am the sheriff!" The final days of our father were not ones to repeat. My youngest sister lived next door to my father. Her husband, a doctor, who had fetched his stethoscope and pronounced his death, once said that the best way to die was instantly, with no forethought or expectation, no sense of days passing as you succumbed. And of course that is not a dailiness I recommend to anyone, though such a dailiness may be inevitable for some of us. For the living, however, dailiness becomes attendance as the loved one departs. It becomes watchful and loving vigilance as one who was part of your daily life ceases to be. The living remain conscious of the one they have lost, even though that one has left consciousness altogether.

The essays that follow are about poetry and the making of poetry and in a couple of cases, the makers of poetry, and the way poetry celebrates being alive as an act of consciousness. The imagination may be rooted in whatever we think of as the unconscious, but making a poem, no matter how we might do it, either by writing or speaking, is a deliberate and conscious act. When in the Book of Genesis, God says, "Let there be light," it is like saying let me see what I am making, let me give myself a place where there is time, and think about what I am doing. Let there be poetry—let there be a means to make it. For any believer, like myself, God is the creator. God is the first poet or maker. And God makes the great poem of creation through incomprehensible stretches of time, so great that physicists suggest that time actually is a misleading concept and really does not exist. But in all of our stories about the making of space and time, about creation, the making happens day by day. The work of creation is daily. It is the poetry of daily life.

Dailiness

When the Light Came On

THE EPIC *GILGAMESH*

I f consciousness is a light, that fire Prometheus stole from the
gods and gave to humanity, then surely the light came on long
before the world's oldest epic, *Gilgamesh*, was pressed in cunei-
form figures on clay tablets. And yet we associate consciousness
with language in a profound way, and if *Gilgamesh* is our oldest
epic, both of the East and the West, written down in the third
millennium before the common era, only five thousand years
after the end of the last Ice Age, then it is a record of what first
occurred to human beings as they recognized this remarkable
gift—consciousness—which seemed to set them apart from
the rest of creation. *Gilgamesh*, the epic, is obsessed with consciousness. It is especially obsessed with the consciousness of
death, the individual awareness that one will die, the knowledge that every third thought *is* our grave and cannot help but
be. William James asserted that consciousness was a fact, valid
and irrefutable. *Gilgamesh* reminds us that the consciousness of
death, our death, gives that fact its irrefutable validity.

Many hands have done their part in translating this epic of
Mesopotamia, the region where the Biblical Garden of Eden

was set. The novelist John Gardner, twenty-five years ago, was working on a translation when he died. Thirty years ago, Herbert Mason produced an excellent, highly compressed version. And in 1992, David Ferry brought forth a translation, which Robert Pinsky has referred to as one of the best ever written. Now, Stephen Mitchell, translator of poetry in many languages, has produced a version that requires our attention (*Gilgamesh: A New English Version*).

Gilgamesh is the epic of two heroes, the eponymous Gilgamesh and his bosom friend Enkidu. In his introduction to his translation, Mitchell argues that these two in their actions and message are relevant to contemporary history. He wants his readers to appreciate the significance of publishing a translation of *Gilgamesh*, an ancient epic of Mesopotamia, which is the location of modern day Iraq. He makes sure to remind us that the moral challenges facing Gilgamesh had a subtlety ignored by the United States when it invaded Iraq. One cannot fault the translator for seizing this opportunity. After all, Seamus Heaney in his best-selling translation of *Beowulf* claims it as a Celtic epic, which would ally the great Anglo-Saxon poem more closely with Irish interests. However, Heaney bases his claim on discoveries he made in returning to the Anglo-Saxon studies of his college days. Mitchell can make no such linguistic claims. When he tries to draw parallels between the actions of the heroes, Gilgamesh and Enkidu, and the U.S., the parallels do not make sense. And, truth be told, they are not what interest me.

Despite claims for contemporary relevance, the value of reading *Gilgamesh* is in learning what was on the minds of people who, in the 5,000 years since the Ice Age, had advanced to an agricultural society that had in turn produced the enclosed Eden of the city-state. They wrote, built, governed, crafted their arts, worshiped their gods, and engaged in commerce. They were a civilization, one of the first. What, then, did they still fear? *Gilgamesh* tells us that it was death they primarily feared, but they had other fears, too. The wilderness and the forest frightened them as reminders of where they had come from before they built great cities like Uruk, where the epic begins and ends. *Gilgamesh* shows readers what the ancient Mesopotamians valued. Unlike many another later epic, *Gilgamesh* records no warfare. There is combat, but no clash of armies as a result of peoples vying for dominance and power. The heroes go on their quests as representative individuals rather than extensions of political bodies.

Above all, the ancient Mesopotamians valued civic harmony. The citizens of Uruk are being terrorized by Gilgamesh, their king. He interferes with their wedding rituals and insists that he sleep with every new bride before her husband. The bully has to be tamed and taught to behave. And so friendship, another human good, becomes the means by which out-of-control Gilgamesh is made to behave. The goddess who created Gilgamesh obligingly creates Enkidu. The creation of Enkidu may parallel the creation of Eve in its purpose, so that Gilgamesh may have a companion. Like Adam, Enkidu is made of dust or clay. He is not offered to Gilgamesh as a mate, but as a friend. The women we meet in this world are either goddesses, mothers, or temple prostitutes. But their sexuality has not had the civilizing effect on Gilgamesh that Enkidu's friendship is meant to have. First, however, Enkidu himself, who runs and feeds with wild animals like gazelles, requires civilization. It is sex that is employed to civilize him.

Sex civilizes or it should do so. The ancient Mesopotamians valued it for that reason. The poem suggests that sex with a civilized woman will domesticate the wild man, Enkidu, and therefore indirectly the uncivil Gilgamesh. Enkidu is clearly a type of the green man, living on the margins, reminding us of our origins among the animals. The civilizing of Enkidu requires days of sexual intercourse with the temple prostitute, Shamat. The incredible result is that Enkidu, as a creature of pure animal instinct, easily tempted to enjoy continuous sex until he is surfeited, finds himself more interested in another pursuit. And that pursuit is friendship with Gilgamesh.

Sex, then, may be a threshold to friendship. The homoerotic element to the poem is pronounced. Gilgamesh and Enkidu live in an age when sexual prohibitions have not rigidified. It shouldn't be difficult to explain this to a Western audience that ought to know the story of David and Jonathan in the Bible. The fact is that even today on the streets of many cities in the Middle East, it would not be unusual to see men who are friends holding hands. The West may find this hard to understand. Our polarizing sense of sexuality has scoured away all subtleties in our own culture with regard to friendship.

Sex and friendship are civilizing. That is the message of *Gilgamesh*, a subtle and appropriate one, indeed. When Gilgamesh comes to claim his first night with a recent bride, the newly enfranchised Enkidu is there to stop him. They struggle, and though Gilgamesh wins, he ceases to interfere in any more wedding nights. Enkidu, with remarkable gravity for one who was recently grazing with gazelles, reminds Gilgamesh of his remarkable endowments as a human being and his destiny to rule, and with that, Enkidu and Gilgamesh embrace, kiss, and become like brothers.

Gilgamesh and Enkidu embark on a quest to confront and subdue Humbaba, the spirit of the forest. This is the crucial event of the epic, for after confronting and killing Humbaba, Enkidu's own life is forfeit. It would have been better to let Humbaba be. But I think it is a necessary confrontation, a final break with the wild and uncivilized world from which Enkidu derives. It is debatable whether or not this break was a wise thing. Nevertheless, the story of Enkidu makes it necessary.

On their way Gilgamesh experiences a series of disquieting dreams which Enkidu interprets favorably for him as predicting their victory. After they dispatch Humbaba, it is Enkidu's turn to dream, this time of his own demise. The important role played by dreaming and dream interpretation suggests another value of ancient Mesopotamian life. The dream mirrors consciousness, tricking us into thinking we are awake and conscious while dreaming. The value placed on dreaming has changed through the millennia, but dreaming has never lost its importance. In *Gilgamesh* we see an original belief that dreams were connected with the waking world, and therefore prophetic. We may also infer that dreams provided a reason for believing in the afterlife, even though the afterlife dreamed of by Enkidu, as he anticipates his death, is bleak indeed.

Emperor and clown, master and slave, squatting in dull darkness, are all equal in death. Its leveling power has not diminished in our awareness. Part of Gilgamesh's grief at losing his friend must stem from imagining him in these circumstances for eternity.

But to have no friend or companion is also hard for the mind to bear. As Enkidu ails, Gilgamesh proposes that he make a golden statue in the likeness of his friend. Enkidu responds that it would be futile. Still, after his death, Gilgamesh calls his craftsmen together and orders all the craftsmen of his realm to collect jewels and precious metals and sail them down the Euphrates to the great city of Uruk, there to be fashioned into a monumental statue of Enkidu.

Gilgamesh's urgency to memorialize his friend may be partly to offset the dismal afterlife which Enkidu has already portrayed. But it may also be to acknowledge one of the weaknesses of consciousness. It is hard to hold our absent loved ones in mind without any aid to memory. Gilgamesh may believe an image of Enkidu has curative powers, a notion that Enkidu, always the more enlightened one, knows is false. After all, this is an epic of a region where a great monotheistic faith will arise which distrusts all images. But in this poignant response to loss, a demand of consciousness is again assuaged, while another is exacerbated. Enkidu's death arouses a sense of mortality in Gilgamesh himself. It is strange that he wonders if he must die, too, since that is one of the lessons Enkidu was meant to teach him.

He looks for a new savior, one to whom the gods have granted immortality.

So Gilgamesh goes in search of Utnapishtim, survivor of the Flood, who has eternal life. The first modern readers of *Gilgamesh*, in the mid-nineteenth century, were most excited by its narrative of the Flood, nearly a word-for-word account of the version in Genesis. Mitchell points out that the Gilgamesh Flood narrative is actually much older than the story of Noah's ark, and its point and presentation are different as well. It is a story within a story, narrated by Utnapishtim to Gilgamesh, and in *Gilgamesh* it remains a secret why the gods sent the Flood.

One way to read Gilgamesh's quest is as an expansion of consciousness. On his way to the distant, transoceanic realm where Utnapishtim resides, Gilgamesh encounters one of the most interesting figures in any epic, Shiduri, a goddess of sagacity and mistress of the art of brewing, "who," Mitchell tells us in a note, "keeps a tavern at the edge of the world." Before Gilgamesh sets off on his second quest, she speaks to him like an Akkadian Glinda the Good Witch saying that it would be better to enjoy the life he has, preferably in his own house, with his own family, because human beings were not made to be immortal. Wearing nice clothes, making music and dancing, spending time with your wife and children is the best way to live, she advises. But it may be no way for a hero to live, until of course he has exhausted his heroism.

Gilgamesh learns that Utnapishtim was made immortal because he discovered a secret of the gods—their plan to flood the earth. He built his ark, stowed his family aboard, along with domestic and wild animals, and—an interesting, civilized touch—plenty of artisans and craftsmen. Like Gilgamesh, he had been the king of a great city and had plans to rebuild. After telling Gilgamesh the story, however, he asks Gilgamesh why he might deserve eternal life, for it is not clear that Gilgamesh has learned any secret of the gods. Utnapishtim sets Gilgamesh a test to stay awake for seven days, a feat which Gilgamesh fails almost immediately. Sleep overwhelms him. Consciousness can expand only so far before it is exhausted. Having failed Utnapishtim's test, Gilgamesh also fails to preserve a plant that Utnapisthim leads him to, which contains the secret of youth. He returns to the great walled city of Uruk, empty-handed, a sadder and a wiser man, still mortal but now possibly accepting of Shiduri's sage advice.

Of the epics that will follow *Gilgamesh*—the *Torah*, the *Iliad*, the *Odyssey*, the *Mahabharata*, the *Ramayana*—most of them have to do with the way one culture and its civilization has supplanted another. I would argue that Gilgamesh's quest for eternal life will find its ultimate expression in the Gospel stories of the Christ. But no other epic to come takes consciousness itself as the ultimate aim, the gift and secret of the gods. Gilgamesh wants to know the secret of eternal life. And since we associate consciousness with identity, we can imagine that to him and our forebears of 5,000 years ago, the secret of eternal life meant to continue as we are, to be who we are, enjoying our lives forever. Gilgamesh returns to his home, having recognized that human immortality is impossible. This knowledge, the consciousness of death, continues to baffle us. Yet *Gilgamesh* suggests that the knowledge we are going to die, and not the possession of eternal life, is the ultimate gift of the gods.

To Make the Final Unity

METAPHOR'S MATTER AND SPIRIT

M y first encounter with metaphor occurred in Sunday School around 1957 when I was five, with the following parable of Jesus:

Matthew 18:12–14

What do you think? If a man has a hundred sheep, and one of them has gone astray, does he not leave the ninety-nine on the hills and go in search of the one that went astray? And if he finds it, truly, I say to you, he rejoices over it more than over the ninety-nine that never went astray. So it is not the will of my Father who is in heaven that one of these little ones should perish.

Of course, it made an impression on me that God would prefer that not "one of these little ones should perish." I felt personally accounted for. Still, the image of a shepherd, also represented as I recall on a Sunday School poster, with a lamb hung across his shoulders, footing his way down a treacherous slope back to his flock, impressed me, too. I knew the difference between the literal and the figurative; I don't think I am alone in assuming that children are wiser in this regard than, as adults, we think they are. Besides, the parable—the word itself means "comparison"—provides the mirror between its two parts at "So . . ." What fascinated me was not that there was a parallel between the A part of the metaphor, God's concern for his human souls, and the B part of the metaphor, a shepherd's concern for his flock of sheep, but the actual physical activity of finding a lost sheep in mountainous terrain and that the remaining flock would even hang around as said shepherd went looking for his stray sheep or lamb. The long-ago-viewed poster showed a stalwart shepherd of Judea, dressed in a practical, striped djellaba, with a lamb or young sheep draped across his shoulders, making his way back to his flock. The reality of the metaphor caught my attention. The actuality that it presented was not simply an illustration. Shepherds really did go out and round up their strays. The poster vouched for it. The biblical text suggested that nothing was unusual about such a search. Jesus was the most down to earth and relevant of poets. He drew every metaphor from his listeners' experience.

But why make a metaphor in the first place? What is it meant to accomplish? Jesus made them to provide a practical foundation for profound moral lessons and mysteries. His metaphors are didactic, based on the experience of his listeners. At times they are as paradoxical as koans. Metaphors give us, as poets, great pleasure. Does it make sense to ask whether our intent in making them is secular or religious? I suspect metaphor remains religious in a vestigial and reliquary way. I will try to describe why I think so. I also think metaphors derive their power by an inexactitude. At the point where we realize that in the transfer of qualities from A to B, there is reality in each part that will not go, refusing to be either figurative or literal. In the end God is God, a shepherd is a shepherd, and the energy of the comparison derives from its breakdown, from what each part withholds from the other. We may wish to think of God as a shepherd so the metaphor comes into being. But the power of the metaphor resides in what cannot be compared in God or shepherd.

St. Paul is a very good poet, not a great poet like Jesus, but he's a close second. He invents Christianity through metaphor and his best metaphor for the promise of belief occurs in his famous first letter to the Corinthians, in chapter 13, verse 12:

For now we see through a glass darkly; but then face to face: now I know in part; but then shall I know even as also I am known.

βλέπομεν γὰρ ἄρτι δι᾽ ἐσόπτρου ἐν αἰνίγματι, τότε δὲ πρόσωπον πρὸς πρόσωπον·ἄρτι γινώσκω ἐκ μέρους, τότε δὲ ἐπιγνώσομαι καθὼς καὶ ἐπεγνώσθην.

To make a point about a preposition, I have included the New Testament or Koine Greek that St. Paul wrote. The English passage is from the King James Authorized Version, a passage subsequent translations have rendered as "For now we see in a mirror dimly, but then face to face, etc." The idea of seeing *through* that glass or mirror is more compelling and truer to me than is the metaphor of seeing "in" it. The word "glass" suggests a transparency which "mirror" does not. Apparently the Greek bears me out; a colleague who reads New Testament Greek has told me that the preposition "dia," the fourth word in the Greek passage, is closer to "through" than to "in." This passage is crucial for my sense of metaphor and what I seek in metaphor. Metaphor not only reflects likeness, but also accesses likeness. We do not wish only to see an apt correspondence, a similitude. We want a reality that will equal the reality we have realized, a reality that can only be described in this way. At some level we want the reflection of likeness and the access to likeness to be the same; this may be why the basic formula for metaphor is not A is like B, but A *is* B. If I sound as if I am verging on Marianne Moore's famous requirement for "imaginary gardens with real toads in them," then give me a little time.

To make a metaphor is always the greatest and most exciting risk in a poem. To fail at it can be almost as exhilarating as to succeed. James Dickey believes the central metaphor of Matthew Arnold's "Dover Beach" (1867) doesn't work, as grand as it is. It doesn't matter if he is right (I don't think he is). But in suspecting the accuracy of Arnold's metaphor, Dickey has inferred what I think may be a problem with all metaphors, especially the most effective and powerful.

Dover Beach

The sea is calm tonight,
The tide is full, the moon lies fair
Upon the straits; on the French coast the light
Gleams and is gone; the cliffs of England stand,
Glimmering and vast, out in the tranquil bay.
Come to the window, sweet is the night air!
Only, from the long line of spray
Where the sea meets the moon-blanched land,
Listen! you hear the grating roar
Of pebbles which the waves draw back, and fling,
At their return, up the high strand,
Begin, and cease, and then again begin,
With tremulous cadence slow, and bring
The eternal note of sadness in.

Sophocles long ago
Heard it on the Aegean, and it brought
Into his mind the turbid ebb and flow
Of human misery; we
Find also in the sound a thought,
Hearing it by this distant northern sea.

The Sea of Faith
Was once, too, at the full, and round earth's shore
Lay like the folds of a bright girdle furled.
But now I only hear
Its melancholy, long, withdrawing roar,
Retreating, to the breath

Of the night wind, down the vast edges drear
And naked shingles of the world.

Ah, love, let us be true
To one another! for the world, which seems
To lie before us like a land of dreams,
So various, so beautiful, so new,
Hath really neither joy, nor love, nor light,
Nor certitude, nor peace, nor help for pain;
And we are here as on a darkling plain
Swept with confused alarms of struggle and flight,
Where ignorant armies clash by night.

To me this is a poem of surpassing greatness. In these days I feel we are swept by "alarms of struggle and flight / Where ignorant armies clash by night." I think our only recourse is to put faith in one another. But is there a problem with the poem's central metaphor? Here's what James Dickey as critic claims:

> The one difficulty of the poem, it seems to me, is in the famous third strophe wherein the actual sea is compared to the Sea of Faith. If Arnold means that the Sea of Faith was formerly at high tide, and he hears now only the sound of the tide going out, one cannot help thinking also of the cyclic nature of tides, and the consequent coming of another high tide only a few hours after the present ebb. In other words, the figure of speech appears valid only on one level of the comparison; the symbolic half fails to sustain itself. Despite the magnificence of the writing in this section, I cannot help believing that it is the weakest part of the poem when it should be the strongest; the explicitness of the comparison seems too ready-made. Yet I have the poem as it is so deeply in memory that I cannot imagine it changed, and would not have it changed even if I knew it would be a better poem thereby. ("Arnold, 'Dover Beach,'" *Babel to Byzantium*)

Here Dickey sounds like Marianne Moore's "literalist of the imagination"; he wants that toad, Arnold's "Sea of Faith," to be real. Considering the tidal resurgence of religious faith in the century and a half since Arnold invented this metaphor which Dickey finds to be flawed, Arnold had the gift of prophecy. Possibly Arnold, if he were thinking as Dickey does, was actually hopeful that the Sea of Faith would be at the full once again, though what would Arnold think about those passionately intense about their faith today? Arnold's great metaphor derives exactly from his situation; the risk he runs and possibly fails at is exactly the one Dickey has indicated. I believe Arnold has seen through to a reality that makes sense in a way that Arnold's current situation does not. Metaphor is the product of a more sensible and unified reality. Dickey objects to the Sea of Faith as a metaphor because it does not wholly make sense and is not wholly unified, but it comes close. To quote Robert Frost, "Let's be precise. But not too precise."

Perhaps to succeed, metaphor has to fail in some way in order to reflect the lack of unity it brings with it from the world. When Arnold claims that Sophocles heard what he is hearing, "long ago" on the Aegean, he is calling to mind the following passage from *Antigone*, wherein the Chorus comments on the problems faced by the family of Oedipus:

> Blest are they whose days have not tasted of evil. For when a house hath once been shaken from heaven, there the curse fails nevermore, passing from life to life of the race; even as, when the surge is driven over the darkness of the deep by the fierce breath of Thracian sea-winds, it roils up the black sand from the depths, and there is a sullen roar from wind-vexed headlands that front the blows of the storm. (583–91, trans. Sir Richard C. Jebb)

Sophocles draws his comparison specifically between a storm and the ill-fated family. Arnold extends it to refer to human misery generally, and changes the terms from storm—"the surge"—to tide—"ebb and flow." He breaks the connection of Sophocles' metaphor to make his own.

Metaphor as a corrective or as a more accurate alternative to incorrect thinking is present in W. H. Auden's comparison of poetry to a river in "In Memory of W. B. Yeats" (1941). In a sense he is speaking to and correcting himself, for he has understood that poetry cannot affect historical events, even as he appears to address W. B. Yeats, a poet who suspected his work had an effect on events of the Irish Civil War.

> You were silly like us; your gift survived it all:
> The parish of rich women, physical decay,
> Yourself. Mad Ireland hurt you into poetry.
> Now Ireland has her madness and her weather still,
> For poetry makes nothing happen: it survives
> In the valley of its making where executives
> Would never want to tamper, flows on south
> From ranches of isolation and the busy griefs,
> Raw towns that we believe and die in; it survives,
> A way of happening, a mouth.

Poetry is not an agent of change but a phenomenon in itself, subject to change but unaffected by the very agents who might turn its course or dam it up. To embody poetry in a natural phenomenon like a river, especially one that empties into the sea, to say it is "a way of happening" reminds us of how profoundly such a feature of the landscape *can* affect history. While Auden limits the claims for poetry as a historical agent, he expands its reach as part of history. Yes, there is a point where the metaphor's unity breaks down; it is at that mouth where the river ceases to exist and empties into the sea, which for Auden always represented disorder. But if the river ceases to exist at that point, does poetry? Poetry needs a mouth to utter it, even to bring it into being: that is its way of happening. The mouth where the river empties itself of its identity is the mouth that makes poetry. Could it be that at the point where the metaphor breaks down, the greatest energy is released?

I have another religious text in mind. In book VII, part X of his *Confessions*, St. Augustine, who was captivated by St. Paul's image of the dark mirror, says to God, "I perceived myself to be far from thee, in the region of unlikeness." Life for St. Augustine could be lived in one of two realms, the realm of likeness to Christ or a realm too far from Christ to be at all like Him, that is, the region of unlikeness. This realistic, metaphorical thinking might seem alien to us, but Robert Frost had this kind of thinking in mind when he said, in "Education by Poetry," "Greatest of all attempts to say one thing in terms of another is the philosophical attempt to say matter in terms of spirit, spirit in terms of matter, to make the final unity." "That is," he said, "the greatest attempt that ever failed." St. Augustine would say that failure is the reason for Grace. We might say it is the reason for poetry.

We make metaphors in order to achieve what W. H. Auden called "the restored relation." I know that to suggest as much emphasizes that religious aspect of metaphor, a vestige that I am trying not to insist on, because it is offputting to those who are not religious and who suspect that entire frame of reference. One of my favorite poets is a fellow preacher's kid who spent most of his career abjuring the religiosity of his childhood and the entire Christian faith, especially the brand of Presbyterianism he grew up with. Frankly, I think it is impossible to deny your intellectual foundations, no matter how shaky you believe they are or how corrupt. W. S. Merwin, in poem after poem, looks through the dark glass to a completion, a restored relation, by means of metaphor. I think he accomplishes that, too, more often than not. But I want to look at a poem, from *The Moving Target* (1963), in which the metaphor breaks down in a dynamic way.

The Present

The walls join hands and
It is tomorrow:

The birds clucking to the horses, the horses
Doing the numbers for the hell of it,
The numbers playing the calendars,
The saints marching in,
It seems only yesterday,
                    when what
I keep saying to myself is
Take a leaf from the fire, open
Your hand, see
Where you are going,
When what I am trying to find is
The beginning,
In the ashes,
A wing, when what we are looking for
In each other
Is each other,

The stars at noon,

While the light worships its blind god.

This poem begins strongly, with what Robert Bly might have called a "deep image": "The walls join hands and / It is tomorrow." Time and space meet, as they do in perspective, are personified, and an apt metaphor shows how the two affect each other, how it is possible to think of one in terms of the other. After that, the poem wanders through a menagerie of diction and surreal relationships, which seems to be the result of tomorrow's arrival. The poet hopes to capture the present, to find a metaphor for it, a much harder task than finding images for the past and future. To quote Frost again, "the present is too present to imagine." Merwin makes a sidetrack into "The Four Quartets," as he searches for "the beginning / In the ashes," but then he finds an excitement that ascends in intensity. To capture the present in a metaphor is as much as to say "what we are looking for / In each other / Is each other, // The stars at noon."

What is the present? It is "the stars at noon," space hidden in time. *Heavy*, as we might have said in the sixties, when the poem was published, and I don't mean that entirely facetiously. The beauty and the breakdown of this metaphor comes in the poem's final line: "While the light worships its blind god." As right as this seems as a metaphor for our searching, its effect is to undermine the attempt to make a unity. Our yearning response to our flawed intelligence causes us to adore the sun, a god that has no consciousness of its effect. "The stars at noon." What a great metaphor for what we search for in each other and for the present itself! But remember it's just a metaphor.

The gaze through the dark glass described by St. Paul seeks the completion of identity, to know oneself as one has been known. My own Christianity may raise all kinds of alarms as I try to explain what I think leads a poet to make a metaphor—to look through the dark glass to clarity—which also means to recognize a unified self, a restored relation. But Christianity is not the only faith or philosophy that holds out this kind of atonement as ultimately desirable. In making a metaphor the poet acts on that same impulse toward unity, the restoration of relation. One of the beauties of metaphor is its promise of putting a fragmented self back together. One of its dynamic and exciting issues is the way that promise isn't quite kept. Here's a poem in which a poet imagines remaking himself as a way of demonstrating the healing power of metaphor.

Let Me Begin Again

Let me begin again as a speck
of dust caught in the night winds
sweeping out to sea. Let me begin
this time knowing the world is
salt water and dark clouds, the world
is grinding and sighing all night, and dawn
comes slowly and changes nothing. Let
me go back to land after a lifetime

of going nowhere. This time lodged
in the feathers of some scavenging gull
white above the black ship that docks
and broods upon the oily waters of
your harbor. This leaking freighter
has brought a hold full of hayforks
from Spain, great jeroboams of dark
Algerian wine and quill pens that can't
write English. The sailors have stumbled
off toward the bars of the bright houses.
The captain closes his log and falls asleep.
1/10'28. Tonight I shall enter my life
after being at sea for ages, quietly,
in a hospital named for an automobile.
The one child of millions of children
who has flown alone by the stars
above the black wastes of moonless waters
that stretched forever, who has turned
golden in the full sun of a new day.
A tiny wise child who this time will love
his life because it is like no other.

Philip Levine, from 7 Years from Somewhere (1979)

The poet is asking to be born again, not in the Holy Spirit and not as someone else, but as himself. The metaphor, however, is an old one, alienation as a sense of being at sea, here recast as a return to land. The poet is an unlikely cargo, a speck in a gull's wing which somehow makes the transition to the harbor and the hospital where Levine was born on January 10, 1928, as noted in the captain's log. The promise the poet makes is like the promise everyone who has ever asked for another chance has made, including those twice born in the bosom of Jesus. Once again the metaphor derives its greatest power from the moment it breaks down. Why will the "tiny wise child" love his life this time? Not because of likeness, not because of the transcendence offered to that passage through the dark glass to the unified reality on the other side, but because of unlikeness, an insistence on separateness, uniqueness. Our tiny wise child of a reborn poet is going to love his life "this time"—why?— "because it is like no other."

When Alice made her passage through the looking glass into its mystery, she found irony, riddle, and paradox. Denise Levertov finds role reversal.

She and the Muse

Away he goes, the hour's delightful hero,
arrivederci: and his horse clatters
out of the courtyard, raising
a flurry of straw and scattering hens.

He turns in the saddle waving a plumed hat,
his saddlebags are filled with talismans,
mirrors, parchment histories, gifts and stones,
indecipherable clues to destiny.

He rides off in the dustcloud of his own
story, and when he has vanished she
who had stood firm to wave and watch
from the top step, goes in to the cool

flagstoned kitchen, clears honey and milk and bread
off the table, sweeps from the hearth
ashes of last night's fire, and climbs the stairs
to strip tumbled sheets from her wide bed.

       Now the long-desired
visit is over. The heroine
is a scribe. Returned to solitude,
eagerly she re-enters the third room,

the room hung with tapestries, scenes that change
whenever she looks away. Here is her lectern,

here her writing desk. She picks a quill,
dips it, begins to write. But not of him.

From Candles in Babylon (1982)

Metaphor makes sense in a way the real world does not. It can also be a form of pastoral when it creates a world we might prefer to the world we inhabit. Here everything bespeaks a world of Renaissance authenticity, the heightened reality of a Vermeer—the horse, the courtyard, the saddlebags with their treasures, the flagstoned kitchen, the hearth, the tapestries—all that is missing is servants, the ones we know would actually be cleaning up as the woman repairs to her writing room. But this is part of the set up: The poet clues us in since the Cavalier plume in the hero's hat as he gallops off into the mystery of his own story matches the quill in the heroine's hand as she begins to write. The poet has seduced us into the Cavalier world, a costume drama in a favorite epoch, the pre-industrial, colorful seventeenth century, when poets like Richard Lovelace took leave of their Lucastas for the sake of honor. In other words, a male fantasy, in which our hero may believe he has enjoyed an hour with his muse, and rides off deluded to think the poem and the story are his, when in fact the roles are reversed.

But the poem is better than that, because of the way that metaphor breaks down. Post-modern hints exist, including those shape-shifting tapestries and the idea of the "third room," surely the room of her own required by Virginia Woolf. The dynamic breakdown of the metaphor comes not in the satisfying role reversal: the woman poet derives creative energy from her male muse but does not write about him, so showing no more fidelity than male poets have in the same circumstances. After all Lovelace takes his leave of Lucasta because, as he proclaims, he loves honor more. The metaphor breaks down when we realize that he—the departed "hour's delightful hero"—may not be our heroine's muse at all, in fact, probably is no more than a diversion. We are not permitted to see the actual encounter with her muse, only the situation in which it occurs and her initial posture as she begins to write. We travel through time via metaphor from the boudoir of Amber St. Clare in Kathleen Winsor's *Forever Amber* to the bedroom of Emily Dickinson in Adrienne Rich's "Vesuvius at Home."

A poem by Michelle Boisseau wonderfully illustrates the matter and spirit of metaphor, for not only does it provide us a metaphor whose reality in relation to its subject is tangible, believable, and sensible, but the poem also shows the inchoate and disordered pieces of a life that metaphor may unify. Here we get both sides of the dark looking glass.

Time Done Is Dark
—Archibald MacLeish

Childhood is a nicked black trunk
you move when you move, from attics
to basements, storage shed, crawl space,
walk-in closet. When they were in

their sixties and their mother in
her eighties, they said to her, We
are miserable, our childhoods
were miserable. And their mother?

Oldest of seventeen, four years
of school, Nothing Soup—raw milk, salt,
pepper, flour—spring snow sparking
through the wallboards, her first child

at fifteen. Childhood is a nicked
trunk you don't have to look inside
to remember. Blasted lining,
the smell of nickels. Childhood, let

it be long ago, like glaciers.

Michelle Boisseau, from *Poetry* (November 2005)

Why make a metaphor except to try to embody disembodied and disunified experience, to make something of that "Nothing Soup," the metaphor at the heart of the metaphor in this poem. Barely contained in that nicked black trunk of childhood is the mother's life, lapping over from stanza three into stanza four with its wrenching detail about having her first child "at fifteen." Why were the children, now old people, miserable in their childhoods? I hear two other poems about sources here, W. B. Yeats's "The Circus Animals Desertion" and Philip Larkin's "This Be the Verse," but Boisseau's makes Yeats's "foul rag and bone shop of the heart" and Larkin's deepening "coastal shelf" of misery seem rather grand by comparison to her nicked black trunk and nothing soup. That childhood is a trunk and not a more contemporary cardboard box attests to its durability; no matter how many times it moves with us, no matter the inner wear—that "blasted lining"—the most it is going to suffer is a few nicks. The trunk is durable, with an heirloom's intimacy and unsentimental value, and in this poem contains the Mother's own childhood deprivations, including its stark brevity. That tantalizing "Nothing Soup" may be the metaphor for what we all begin with when we make a metaphor, meager elemental ingredients—like the raw milk, salt, pepper, and flour, the food of the deprived.

The poem's turn from metaphor to simile produces the excitement, the point where the breakdown gives off the most energy. The trunk image suffices only too well as it brings together the disparate elements of misery that the poet associates with childhood. "Childhood," the poem ends, "let // it be long ago, like glaciers." We've already had a hint of the wintry in "spring snow sparking / through the wallboards" and of the geological, in the "smell of nickels," even in that "blasted lining," so "glaciers" don't exactly come out of nowhere. And yet they are not related spatially to childhood; rather they are temporal: let them stand for the long ago, so that childhood may be associated with them, let childhood be like the Ice Age, long past, of which glaciers are remnants. The final simile is rough—not parallel, for one childhood we have glaciers innumerable—and dissonant, but tonally exactly right. Yes, the nicked black trunk is too close, too right for childhood; let it be like something else we don't carry with us. In the breakdown, an emotional energy is released, like the smoke of dry ice.

The poem's title is from the prologue to Archibald MacLeish's 1932 epic *Conquistador*, based on Bernal Díaz's history of the conquest of Mexico, *The Conquest of New Spain*. In the prologue MacLeish exhorts the spirits of Cortez and his men to come to him without their historical identities, but as they were in life. "Time done is dark as are sleep's thickets," he writes, "Dark is the past: none waking walk there." Boisseau has added to a complaint about the obscurity of history, a tone of ratification. The past is dark? Then let it be—dark and far off.

If it sounds too religious to call metaphor an incarnation, then let's call it a manifestation, for it makes available to the senses the intangible, invisible, unknown, obscure; metaphor brings to light, it reveals, it unifies the fragmented, it is an act of making, indeed, like a poem itself. This is not to imply that the metaphor comes to us as the embodiment of goodness: the withdrawing Sea of Faith and the nicked black trunk of childhood are hardly desirable. The act of creation is desirable and, paradoxically, so is the failure or breakdown that must occur for us to recognize the figurative. St. Augustine's region of likeness is literal, in so far as it is real. We have long understood that we cannot live there, that we don't live there. We expect to see *in* the mirror, not *through* the glass, at least in poetry. We no longer live in the garden, which Milton's angel Raphael assured Adam and Eve was the shadow of heaven. We can usually locate in our own lives, our growing up, a point at which our thinking abandoned the figurative. It may be recognizing that rupture between the imaginary and the real and bringing the rupture to life in metaphor that gives metaphor its power as it breaks down. In the following poem, from Chase Twichell's book *Dog*

Language (2005), the poet locates that former way of thinking and its end, without any sentimental yearning. We do not
hear any Wordsworthian lament for a lost world view because
the world is too much with us. Instead we recognize that it is
lost, possibly for the better, even as we remember the glamor of
a time when our parents seemed like divine beings.

The Myths

Italy and Greece lay in ruins,
inhabited by beasts: the Minotaur
in his labyrinth, the *scrush* of his hide
against its walls; the blinded Cyclops
groping for Ulysses among the sheep.
Dad taught us all the myths.

Up on Mount Olympus
people disguised themselves
as animals. It was like that then.
It's not like that now.
Back then you were half animal
if your father was a god.

No, it's not like that now, but that inspired coinage, "*scrush*," to
imagine the beast as he prowls his labyrinth, rubbing against
the walls in a gesture full of pathos both for its naturalistic accuracy and for its hint of weariness, boredom, and sadness. The
dynamic breakdown of Twichell's metaphor begins in line two
of stanza two. The gods who lived "Up on Mount Olympus" are
referred to as people, which is odd, who "disguised themselves /
as animals." But what she catches here is the child's apprehension of the myths, especially as they are relayed by Ovid, who
portrays divine behavior as all too human. In this poem the
word "animal" recalls its origin in *anima* or soul and is synonymous with human. The transition works by analogy, "gods disguised themselves as people," "people disguised themselves as

animals." One hears the parental voice assuring the children, "It was like that then," but don't worry, "It's not like that now." The retrospective voice lends ambiguity to "Back then": the past of myth, the past of childhood. Back then you were half animal or human, if you were the child of a god and one of the mortals he had loved. Back then you felt like an animal, at least half of one, ensouled and embodied, because your father seemed like a god. Or possibly you felt like a monster, like the Minotaur, child of a human and an animal, specifically Pasiphae, wife of Minos, and a sacrificial bull she was made to love by Neptune. Look how complicated this implication becomes when delved into. It is rather terrible to consider, like many of the images of Lowell's *Life Studies* (the book that stands behind many of the poems in Twichell's *Dog Language*), and is radioactive with the joining and splitting of a metaphor as it seeks and just fails to make the final unity of matter and spirit.

In Il Postino, Mario Ruoppolo, the fisherman turned postman and aspiring poet, asks Pablo Neruda if it is possible that the world itself is a metaphor for something else. Neruda, bemused, says he'll have to think about it. But the time when we thought that is far off, like glaciers.

And yet, and yet. When we make a metaphor, we are making that world, and we test metaphors, even the most outlandish, against the world we know, the one which in itself lacks the meaning and unity of metaphor. And it is possible, in fact likely, that the impulse to make metaphor occurs when we do see that world as a metaphor for something else. To tell the truth, I think poets are secret Augustinians, or at least let's say they have one foot in the region of unlikeness and one foot in the region of likeness, and frequently have trouble telling the difference. There's the excitement. There's the origin of our metaphor making. To straddle these realms, as I have done in this essay, is a tenuous condition at best. When a poet makes a metaphor, is it an attempt to put things back together, as things are not found in reality? I don't think metaphor really can put things back together; it is the attempt itself, as it breaks down, that unites matter and spirit, and reminds us why the attempt is made.

Robert Frost's late poem "Directive" acknowledges the impulse to put things back together and the dynamic breakdown that occurs because we cannot. In "Directive" the poet serves as a guide, "who only has at heart [our] getting lost," who leads us to "a house that is no more a house, / Upon a farm that is no more a farm, / And in a town that is no more a town." And once we get there, to that place which is no place now, we are told our actual destination is a brook which still flows there and invited to "Drink and be whole again beyond confusion." We have been promised one destination, only to be offered another; everything we encounter is broken, made simple by the loss of detail, and impossible to restore, and the poem ends only with the directive that we drink; we cannot know if the promised restoration to wholeness will be achieved. It's a great poem, and it performs much of what I have been talking about, with a foot in the land of likeness—the past restored—and a foot in the land of unlikeness—the present in ruins.

But I want to look at a lesser poem by Frost, earlier than "Directive," also a flirtation with allegory, which conveys metaphorically the importance of withholding, of not giving over completely, of not making the final unity.

I Could Give All to Time

To Time it never seems that he is brave
To set himself against the peaks of snow
To lay them level with the running wave,
Nor is he overjoyed when they lie low,
But only grave, contemplative and grave.

What now is inland shall be ocean isle,
Then eddies playing round a sunken reef
Like the curl at the corner of a smile;

And I could share Time's lack of joy or grief
At such a planetary change of style.

I could give all to Time except—except
What I myself have held. But why declare
The things forbidden that while the Customs slept
I have crossed to Safety with? For I am There,
And what I would not part with I have kept.

In all of the poems I have been talking about, time has been the divider, the mirror surface, the untransparent transparency. Frost's acknowledges this more forthrightly than the others. To see through the glass face to face and to be known is to win through to eternity. To give all to time, as Frost says, may be a necessary condition in this passage, but we don't want to do it, because it is a leap of faith. The more human action is to withhold from time what is most precious to us. Time is nicely and allegorically personified in this poem as a leveller without any emotion, certainly without joy or grief, simply laying waste because that is what it does. The metaphor changes marvelously and magically in line 12, with the same kind of spatial dimension that Merwin provides in "The Present." Now it is a matter of crossing borders, hiding what we might have to declare, and concealing in the relative pronoun *what* the secret that the metaphor, if more fully developed, might reveal.

In 1942, when the poem was published in his book *A Witness Tree*, Robert Frost had much to account for: The death of his wife, two of his adult children (Carol and Marjorie), and the mental illness of one (Irma). That he would withhold an essential part of his metaphor, keeping it to himself, is understandable, but it is also, I think, why this shift to a metaphor that breaks down is so powerful and moving. His metaphor of time as a reaper without joy or grief, affecting planetary changes we know to be in progress at this moment (Frost looks like a prophet here, doesn't he?), is very terrible, mitigated only by the old poet's tendency toward whimsy, that "planetary change of style." Though that whimsy is a flaw in some of his poems, here it offsets the grand metaphor of time with one more emotionally accurate—passing through customs with our most precious possessions—a metaphor that is more unifying of matter and spirit, a metaphor for our secrets which must never be shared, but only hinted at, gestured to, kept personal, lest they lose their value.

I assume that all poets love metaphor, and I assume that the opportunity to make a metaphor is one no poet would pass up, even if it meant that the metaphor would fail in some way. I hope my point is clear: to be a successful metaphor, a good metaphor, it must fall short, just as Frost has said. But it must do so in a dynamic way.

Dennis Sampson's book *Needlegrass* (2005) includes a sequence of poems with a rather scary title, "What the Rising of the Dead Shall Mean," which is actually a meditation on the way relationships change, especially among family members, and how death affects memory. The final poem in the sequence records a moment when the poet recognizes that the world may, indeed, be a metaphor for something else, and offers a response to that recognition.

I remember how it was in the darkening twilight.
How the sky took on a luster behind the bluffs
just as the sun went down beyond the river.
One idea—that everything falls away, is lost—
shocked me, although I was just a kid looking at a river
throwing a flat rock off the water. You think
all sorts of things when you're a kid looking at a river.
You keep them until the day arrives when you finally
waken into a world you never thought possible: the horizon's
stained scarlet and the long reach of clouds, the wind
beginning to speak forcefully in the cottonwoods. One idea.
Nothing lasts. Not even the silent river at your feet.

Not that first star directly overhead in a firmament
turning light to dark—turning aquamarine.
And you let that truth come at you. You let it sing.

When I was a freshman in college, I had the opportunity
to speak to the poet Charles Simic after he gave a reading and
to ask him how he had managed, in his poem "Stone," to picture the inner world and cosmology of a pebble. He turned to
me and said, "One takes these things on faith." It was the right
thing to say to me when I was 18, and it is the very thing Sampson demonstrates at the end of his poem. A point comes, when
making a poem, when making metaphor, when you must let the
truth come at you as if you were facing the emerging clarity of
St. Paul's dark mirror. You have to take it on faith that what you
see there is for real.

The Story of a Feeling

It is a mystery why repetition both pleases and bores us. In ritual and liturgy, it reminds and consoles; it brings a former reality again and again into the present, as Passover and Christ's last meal with his disciples do. In song, repetition can also recall the past and give pleasure in returning the listener to the memorable and familiar; as Brian Wilson says, "Let's get together and do it again." In sex, it almost goes without saying, "Once is not enough." But all of these things, ritual, song, and sex, can bore us with the very qualities that please us. So Orsino, as he begins *Twelfth Night*, perfectly articulates the pleasure and the boredom of repetition.

> If music be the food of love, play on,
> Give me excess of it; that, surfeiting,
> The appetite may sicken and so die—
> That strain again;—it had a dying fall;
> O, it came o'er my ear like the sweet south,
> That breathes upon a bank of violets,
> Stealing, and giving odour.—Enough; no more;
> 'Tis not so sweet now as it was before.

In the Gospel of St. Matthew Jesus warns his disciples not to use "vain repetitions" when they pray, thinking they will be heard for "much speaking." He goes on to teach them the most repeated prayer in Christian liturgy. We want variation with ritual, song, and sex—sometimes. At other times, faced with a reality that may be more than we can bear, we want the same old song. At the end of *Waiting for Godot*, Vladimir, struggling to put on his boots and facing another spell of waiting, declares, "Habit is a great deadener." Like all repeated modes of being and artifice, habit beguiles the time until the Messiah comes.

The repetition which numbs our spirits can lift them, too. It reminds us of eternity, when pleasures will never cease, and there will be no more need for repetition; as St. Augustine assures us at the end of *The City of God*, "There we shall rest and see, see and love, love and praise. This is what shall be in the end without end." Repetition underscores the temporal, where we exist; Theodore Roethke, in his villanelle "The Waking," states several times, "I wake to sleep, and take my waking slow. / I learn by going where I have to go." Repetition offers itself to the obsessive, when we can't stand anymore. Think of those repetitions in the poems of Sylvia Plath, culminating in her triumphant declaration, "Daddy, daddy, you bastard, I'm through." Repetition lends itself to parody; remember the Bellman in Lewis Carroll's "The Hunting of the Snark," crying, "What I tell you three times is true." And repetition leads us to the pleasures of variation; I think of all kinds of moments in the poetry of Elizabeth Bishop, including "Invitation to Miss Marianne Moore": "Come like a light in the white mackerel sky, / come like a daytime comet / with a long unnebulous train of words." But I also think more of the ending of Donald Justice's "Ralph: A Love Story": "It was like dying. / No, it *was* dying." Without repetition, there would be no music; without music, there would be no dance or verse, or an idea of either. Imagine the blues without repetition. Impossible.

And yet the blues takes me back to my first point. Although

there is pleasure in restating our feelings and retelling their story, especially with a variation or a difference, nevertheless unceasing sorrow can be monotonous and even maddening. Suffering for too long, as Yeats has implied, can make a stone of the heart—one that doesn't beat, that no longer keeps time through repetition. Responding, perhaps, to Yeats's line, Anthony Hecht writes at the end of his poem "Claire de Lune": "The pain in the drunken singing is your pain. / Morning will taste of bitterness again. / The heart turns to a stone, but it endures." Repetition in poetry helps to tell the story of such feelings. Its purpose, erotic, ritualistic, and mnemonic, is to do more than emphasize.

Coleridge gives the most thoughtful analysis of repetition in poetry. In *Biographia Literaria*, after criticizing Wordsworth's failed attempts to speak the "real language of men," he draws a contrast between kinds of repetition:

> It is indeed very possible to adopt in a poem the unmeaning repetitions, habitual phrases, and other blank counters, which an unfurnished or confused understanding interposes at short intervals, in order to keep hold of his subject, which is still slipping from him, and to give him time for recollection; or in mere aid of vacancy, as in the scanty companies of a country stage the same player pops backwards and forwards, in order to prevent the appearance of empty spaces, in the procession of *Macbeth*, or *Henry VIIIth*. But what assistance to the poet, or ornament to the poem, these can supply, I am at a loss to conjecture. Nothing assuredly can differ either in origin or in mode more widely from the *apparent* tautologies of intense and turbulent feeling, in which the passion is greater and of longer endurance, than to be exhausted or satisfied by a single representation of the image or incident exciting it. Such repetitions I admit to be a beauty of the highest kind. . . .

Those passions greater and longer "than to be exhausted or satisfied by a single representation" he finds in the poetry of the

Bible, and its parallel patterns of statement and reiteration. Here is an example from "The Song of Songs" (2:1–17).

I am the rose of Sharon, and the lily of the valleys.

As the lily among thorns, so is my love among the daughters.

As the apple tree among the trees of the wood, so is my beloved among the sons. I sat down under his shadow with great delight, and his fruit was sweet to my taste.

He brought me to the banqueting house, and his banner over me was love.

Stay me with flagons, comfort me with apples: for I am sick of love.

His left hand is under my head, and his right hand doth embrace me.

I charge you, O ye daughters of Jerusalem, by the roes, and by the hinds of the field, that ye stir not up, nor awake my love, till he please.

The voice of my beloved! Behold, he cometh leaping upon the mountains, skipping upon the hills.

My beloved is like a roe or a young hart; behold, he standeth behind our wall, he looketh forth at the windows, shewing himself through the lattice.

My beloved spake, and said unto me, Rise up, my love, my fair one, and come away.

For, lo, the winter is past, the rain is over and gone;

The flowers appear on the earth; the time of the singing of birds is come, and the voice of the turtle is heard in our land;

The fig tree putteth forth her green figs, and the vines with the tender grape give a good smell. Arise, my love, my fair one, and come away.

O my dove, that art in the clefts of the rock, in the secret places of the stairs, let me see thy countenance, let me hear thy voice; for sweet is thy voice, and thy countenance is comely.

Take us the foxes, the little foxes, that spoil the vines: for our
   vines have tender grapes.
My beloved is mine, and I am his: he feedeth among the lilies.
Until the day break, and the shadows flee away, turn, my
   beloved, and be thou like a roe or a young hart upon the
   mountains of Bether.

There are at least two kinds of passionate repetition present
here. One is obvious, apparently static, yet dynamic, for words
are repeated in a pleasing order but with an incremental difference, as in the chiasmus, "let me see thy countenance, let me
hear thy voice; for sweet is thy voice, and thy countenance is
comely." But the other form of repetition, that of reiteration or
parallel statement, is not so obvious, since the terms change,
"For, lo, the winter is past, the rain is over and gone; the flowers appear on the earth; the time of the singing of birds is come,
and the voice of the turtle is heard in our land." Both forms en-
hance the telling, increasing its dimensions. Both are ways of
expressing love. As the Biblical scholar Francis Landy has ob-
served, "The lover is a stranger who represents . . . the world
that we must make our own."[1] Each new image and metaphor
for the beloved repeats and varies some new knowledge of and
insight into existence. Loving one's lover, in other words, is like
loving the world.

Repetition, restatement, a parallelism that appears static yet
is dynamic, these are techniques that unfold the story of a feeling in Philip Larkin's "Coming."

On longer evenings,
Light, chill and yellow,
Bathes the serene
Foreheads of houses.

1. Francis Landy, "The Song of Songs" in *The Literary Guide to the
Bible*, eds. Alter and Kermode (Harvard University Press, 1987), 305.

A thrush sings,
Laurel-surrounded
In the deep bare garden,
Its fresh-peeled voice
Astonishing the brickwork.
It will be spring soon,
It will be spring soon—
And I, whose childhood
Is a forgotten boredom,
Feel like a child
Who comes on a scene
Of adult reconciling,
And can understand nothing
But the unusual laughter,
And starts to be happy.

At the Iowa Writers' Workshop thirty years ago, some of my classmates and I had a particular fondness for absolute, clarifying statements based on repetition. The end of Randall Jarrell's "90 North," for example: "Pain comes from the darkness / And we call it wisdom. It is pain." Or the end of Weldon Kees's "For My Daughter": "I have no daughter. I desire none." And the final stanza of W. S. Merwin's "The Widow": "This is the waking landscape / Dream after dream after dream walking away through it / Invisible invisible invisible." All endings plangent and rhetorical, even though we usually expressed a dislike for repetition and refrain, or for anything that smacked of the formal lyric. In class once, noting this contradiction in our preferences, Donald Justice offered what he thought was a moving use of repetition, two lines he identified simply as from a poem by Philip Larkin: "It will be spring soon, / It will be spring soon—" I believe the response of the class was something like "Huh?"

When we look at the poem "Coming," we can see that the refrain is both a translation of the bird's astonishing song and the poet's affirmation of its announcement. A bird will usually repeat its song several times; here the effect is to recognize the meaning of its utterance and to affirm it, i.e. "It will be spring soon," says the thrush. "It will indeed," says the poet.

The other pattern of repetition is subtler, and it is a pattern I will be looking for in the other poems I consider. It occurs in the extended simile of the last eight lines.

> And I, whose childhood
> Is a forgotten boredom,
> Feel like a child

Here the word *child*, repeated, has at least two different meanings, and one important effect. To avoid coming right out with the sentimental, "I feel like a child" when I hear a thrush announcing the coming of spring, Larkin inserts the downbeat relative clause, "whose childhood is a forgotten boredom." The meaning of the word *child* in both contexts differs: one is bored, one elated. Or rather, starting to be happy. For the anaphora of "And I," "And can understand," "And starts to be happy" leads us to the approach of happiness, the starting to be different from that bored child. He may have forgotten how it felt to be aroused by the unusual laughter of adults, possibly reconciled by making love, but at the approach of spring, he is reminded. The title "Coming" is repeated in the phrase "who comes on a scene," and its sexual meaning is implied in what the child may be hearing.

One of the excellences of Philip Larkin's poetry is his use of epithets, always fresh and inventive, yet always with a sense of an ageless music, like that bird song, occurring in a modern, suburban setting. Here they are the phrases "Laurel-surrounded" and "fresh-peeled." But these, too, are patterns of repetition since they affect how we hear the other more conventional adjective-noun pairs, "serene foreheads," "forgotten boredom," "adult reconciling," and "unusual laughter."

I mean to invoke John Hollander's figure of echo[2] here, be-cause each more recent poem I have chosen is affected by the echo of the older poem I have paired with it. This is a mode of allusion, as Hollander makes clear. It is entirely possible that Larkin, aficionado of jazz, knew the musical effect of repeating the little refrain in "Coming," but I think the poem is enhanced in every part if we hear the echo of "The Song of Songs" and its sense of the awakening world, both in the wild and in the gar-den, as a time and place when lovers are reconciled.

Certainly the literary echo, along with the other patterns of repetition, affects a reading of Kate Daniels's "Farewell to the Maiden," in light of "The Magnificat" of Mary in the Gospel of St. Luke (1:46–55).

> And Mary said,
> "My soul magnifies the Lord,
> and my spirit rejoices in God my Savior,
> for he has regarded the low estate of his handmaiden.
> For behold, henceforth all generations will call me blessed;
> for he who is mighty has done great things for me,
> and holy is his name.
> And his mercy is on those who fear him
> from generation to generation.
> He has shown strength with his arm,
> he has scattered the proud in the imagination of their hearts,
> he has put down the mighty from their thrones,
> and exalted those of low degree;
> he has filled the hungry with good things,
> and the rich he has sent empty away.
> He has helped his servant Israel,
> in remembrance of his mercy,

2. John Hollander, *The Figure of Echo: A Mode of Allusion in Milton and After* (University of California Press, 1984).

as he spoke to our fathers,
to Abraham and to his posterity for ever."

Mary's soul not only magnifies the Lord, but it magnifies the power of generations, the hope for posterity, the advancement of a people's story into the future. While it is clear that the masculinity of the Lord is also reinforced—the male pronoun is repeated more often than any other word—and the passage ends on a reference to "fathers" and to "Abraham," I think this passage is the story of a feeling; it is the story of Mary's delight in her own posterity: "all generations will call [her] blessed." The great sequence of repetition that pours forth from her, in which she does indeed proclaim the might of a male God, nevertheless corresponds to the unfolding future history that will look back at her with gratitude "for ever."

In contrast to Mary's "Magnificat," in her "Farewell to the Maiden," Kate Daniels emphasizes herself; the personal pronoun is the most repeated word in this poem. And yet if Mary's great hymn is one of submission, in part, to a force greater than her own—to God, but also to generation—then so is Kate Daniels's poem, with a humorous sense of resignation. In Mary's poem, the word becomes flesh. In Daniels's, flesh becomes word or metaphor.

If the body's a text,
this must be the end
of my Bildungsroman.
Heavy with content, my plot
propelled by fate and necessity,
youth is a dream of earlier
chapters. Only flashbacks remain
to the creamy thighs,
unlined neck, the taut
still pond of my maiden's stomach.
Whose subject am I now
but my own? Corners bent, pages

wrinkled, my text is a mess
but original. Once, I wished
to be a verse of gorgeous sinuosity,
a lyric poem, some tightly belted
perfect sonnet or deftly figured
villanelle. Not to be. Bildungsroman
called me in its loud, coarse voice.
That big, fat book that finds its form
simply by following a life.

The extended metaphor of the novel supplies the poem's pat-
terning, its form (an important word in the poem), with reference to content, plot, chapters, flashbacks, subject, pages,
text, and the contrast between the youthful, feminine com-
pression of the lyric poem—of which this poem is an example,
by the way—and the sense that as a Bildungsroman or an extended prose narrative recounting an education, the body has
been defeminized. In fact, the poem appears in a sequence in
the author's *Four Testimonies* (1998) called "Portrait of the Artist as Mother." This poem celebrates the effect of motherhood
on a woman's body, in a more intimate way than "The Magnificat." The pattern of repetition, as it unfolds the extended metaphor, is based on parallelism—that unit of rhythm of so much
of free verse. There are incremental parallel statements: "the
creamy thighs, / unlined neck, the taut / still pond of my maid-
en's stomach." There is the linking of essential words over several lines, e.g. the verb "be" as in "this must be," "I wished to be,"
and "Not to be." And finally there is a metrical parallel between
the phrases "loud, coarse voice" and "big, fat book." Whatever
we hear, it is clear that a deliberate manipulation of rhythm determined by meter can play a useful part. How else does the
final line work its charm except as a pair of dactyls and an ultimate iamb: a pair of falling metrical feet brought up to conclude
by one that rises, and announces the very point of the poem: a
life is affirmed here, accepted and affirmed.

Of course, traditional English verse forms, like the sonnet, can provide a template for meaningful repetition. I am certainly interested in the pattern of repetition of Donne's hybrid sonnet, with its features from both the Italian and the English forms, but what most interests me is the pattern of statement and re-statement, both of phrases and one crucial word.

Holy Sonnet

Why are wee by all creatures waited on?
Why doe the prodigall elements supply
Life and food to mee, being more pure then I,
Simple, and further from corruption?
Why brook'st thou, ignorant horse, subjection?
Why dost thou bull, and bore so seelily
Dissemble weaknesse, and by one mans stroke die,
Whose whole kinde, you might swallow and feed upon?
Weaker I am, woe is mee, and worse then you,
You have not sinn'd, nor need be timorous,
But wonder at a greater wonder, for to us
Created nature doth these things subdue,
But their Creator, whom sin, nor nature tyed,
For us, his Creatures, and his foes, hath dyed.

One creature here asks questions of other creatures, mysti-fied at the hierarchy that separates them, especially since these fellow members of the creation, which the man addresses, are without sin. The octave is made up of questions, each occurring at the A-rhyme, so that we have ?BB??BB?. The "Our Father" in-scribed in the octave rhyme scheme—ABBAABBA—now also becomes, "How can this be? How can this be?" Our speaker in the first quatrain wonders at the servitude of creation as a whole, then in the second quatrain addresses some of the more substantial creatures, the domesticated horse and bull, and the wild boar, who could easily overwhelm a human being, yet suf-fer human domination. Considering their sinlessness, it is a wonder, a prodigy, and it just doesn't seem right. We are on the verge of a Swiftian satire; these in fact are sentiments Swift will later employ at the end of *Gulliver's Travels*. But this is one of John Donne's Holy Sonnets, so the sestet presents us instead with a theological conundrum. Not only has the creation been made for this weaker, unworthy creature, but the creator who is as sinless as any beast of field or forest and less constrained by nature, has given his life for his enemies. Orthodoxy is strained by that "nor nature tyed," for God *has* constrained or tied himself by taking on human nature or form.

The *w*-alliteration of *w*hy and *w*onder ties much together here. (We hear it also in Blake's "The Tyger" and Frost's sonnet "Design.") The parallelism of the questions, with the sense of equality often afforded by this syntax, works with and against the interrogation of hierarchy. The sestet, expressed as a statement, gives a sense of why the questions are asked in the octave, but also brings us to what it means to be a creature of the creation. It reminds us that the very word *creature* implies a creator (just as the word *animal* implies a soul or *anima*). One creature asks questions of another, and ends by suggesting the reason why, as just another member of the creation, he has been endowed with the mysterious ability to ask questions in the first place. Question and answer form the pattern of repetition that tells the story. Only a human being can answer his own questions. It is a poem about the gift of consciousness, as well as the mystery of grace, and how it feels to enjoy both.

The wonder that is greater than the wonder of these animals' subjection is the creator's preference of humankind. Clearly, in an age of bull and bear-baiting (the word *bore* is *beare* in another version of the poem), Donne is not ready to take the next step toward an even more enlightened treatment of his fellow creatures. W. H. Auden, in "In Praise of Limestone," expresses a typically human reservation when he asks "not, please!, to resemble / [t]he beasts who repeat themselves." And yet it is in animal presence that we see soul and consciousness—all that is implied by *anima*—repeated with the most compelling variations. Our regard for our fellow creatures extends at least as far back as when Adam named the animals. It is the story that unfolds in Chase Twichell's "Aisle of Dogs," from her book, *The Ghost of Eden* (1995).

In the first cage
a hunk of raw flesh.
No, it was alive, but skinned.

Or its back was skinned.
The knobs of the spine

poked through the bluish meat.

It was a pit bull, held by the shelter
for evidence until the case
could come to trial,

then they'd put him down. The dog,
not the human whose cruelty

lived on in the brindled body,
unmoving except for the enemy eyes.

Not for adoption, said the sign.

All the other cages held adoptable pets,
the manic yappers, sad matted mongrels,
the dumb slobbering abandoned ones,

the sick, the shaved, the scratching,
the wounded and terrified, the lost,

one to a cage, their water dishes
overturned, their shit tracked around,

on both sides of a long echoey
concrete aisle—clank of chain mesh gates,
the attendant hosing down the gutters

with his headphones on, half-dancing
to the song in his head.

I'd come for kittens. There were none.
So I stood in front of the pit bull's
quivering carcass, its longdrawn death,

its untouched food, its incurable hatred
of my species, until the man with the hose
touched my arm and steered me away,

shaking his head in a way that said
Don't look, Leave him alone.
I don't know why, either.

The title echoes the reference to "The Isle of Dogs" in T. S.
Eliot's *The Waste Land,* which comes at the beginning of the
song of the Thames Maidens. I'm not sure what the poet's intention is, except to suggest that the world of her poem parallels the
world of Eliot's. Twichell shows her suspicion of traditional form
by the altering length of her stanzas in no predictable pattern,
except that the eye tells us quickly they are tercets, couplets, and
single lines. This is a form the poet prefers in many of the poems
in *The Ghost of Eden,* so I am hesitant to draw a particular connection between this form and the poem's subject, except to say
that as the poet looks not only for a reason but for justice, she
keeps seeking an apt unit of lines, and finally settles on tercets.

Certain words in this poem, once they are repeated, accrue
greater meaning by becoming more clearly focused; their repetition parallels the speaker's increasing awareness. We see that
awareness sharpen in the repetitions, "skinned/skinned," "adop-
tion/adoptable," "headphones/head," and even in the ambiguity about referring to the dog as an "it" ("it was alive") or a "him"
("then they'd put him down. The dog, / not the human whose
cruelty // lived on in the brindled body"). The final three tercets take their power from the parallelism established through-

out the poem, allowing for narrative and a listing as evocative as a litany. They give us the poignancy of "it" versus "him" in the last catalogue, "its longdrawn death, // its untouched food, its incurable hatred / of my species." Finally there is the source of human consciousness and morality and all our responsibility: the mind, the brain, in its head, as the attendant, apparently detached with his private music, reaches out to his fellow creature and touches her arm, steering her away, and "shaking his head in a way that said / Don't look, Leave him alone. / I don't know why, either." Imagine if the Grecian Urn had spoken like this to Keats. These three statements, two imperative and one declarative, have equal moral weight of pity and discretion, even as they insist on detachment. Human cruelty is reflected, repeated, in the body of the skinned pit bull. Outrage and impotent wonder are repeated and reflected in the pattern of the poem and the story it unfolds.

I have been referring to story without much reference to narrative, because I have deliberately chosen poems in which narrative is not the point: lyric poems, employing narrative in the most practical ways, as in Larkin's and Twichell's, for setting the scene and taking us through an event in time. But narrative itself in a poem can create that pattern of repetition—a kind of self-consciousness or reflexiveness I suppose I mean—and no poet understood this better than Robert Frost.

"Out, Out—"

The buzz-saw snarled and rattled in the yard
And made dust and dropped stove-length sticks of wood,
Sweet-scented stuff when the breeze drew across it.
And from there those that lifted eyes could count
Five mountain ranges one behind the other
Under the sunset far into Vermont.
And the saw snarled and rattled, snarled and rattled,
As it ran light, or had to bear a load.
And nothing happened: day was all but done.

Call it a day, I wish they might have said
To please the boy by giving him the half hour
That a boy counts so much when saved from work.
His sister stood beside them in her apron
To tell them "Supper." At the word, the saw,
As if to prove saws knew what supper meant,
Leaped out at the boy's hand, or seemed to leap—
He must have given the hand. However it was,
Neither refused the meeting. But the hand!
The boy's first outcry was a rueful laugh,
As he swung toward them holding up the hand
Half in appeal, but half as if to keep
The life from spilling. Then the boy saw all—
Since he was old enough to know, big boy
Doing a man's work, though a child at heart—
He saw all spoiled. "Don't let him cut my hand off—
The doctor, when he comes. Don't let him sister!"
So. But the hand was gone already.
The doctor put him in the dark of ether.
He lay and puffed his lips out with his breath.
And then—the watcher at his pulse took fright.
No one believed. They listened at his heart.
Little—less—nothing!—and that ended it.
No more to build on there. And they, since they
Were not the one dead, turned to their affairs.

The foreshadowing of a dreadful event couldn't be clearer or
more conventionally rendered in the first nine lines, which would
make a perfectly good opening to a piece of naturalistic American fiction from the early twentieth century, except for the way
line three stops us or, rather, waits for us to come back to it.

Sweet-scented stuff when the breeze drew across it.

Everything is in that line. The stuff a life is made of, vividly fragrant and precious, yet hard to describe except as stuff. And cut-

ting through the sibilant sweetness, that "breeze," which both releases the wood's perfume and foreshadows the action of the saw drawing across and ending the boy's life, turning it like the lumber into so much kindling. The z in "breeze" attaches to the z's in "buzzsaw." One pattern of repetition in the poem is resonance, rhyming of image and sound internally. Still, in terms of foreshadowing, the saw will turn the boy to dust, the sunset will end the life of the day and bring darkness down, the repeating mountain ranges—which a student of mine once noticed might be serrated or might suggest serrations as on a saw—will continue in their geographic pattern long, long after the accident.

All of this grows sharper, when the poet interjects himself, aiming this foreshadowing at its inevitable target. It is here, too, that we meet one of the two words most often repeated in the poem: "Call it a day, I wish they might have said / To please the *boy* by giving him the half hour / That a *boy* counts so much when saved from work." We will hear that the saw "Leaped out at the *boy's* hand," we will hear that the "*boy's* first outcry was a rueful laugh," we will hear that "the *boy* saw all," and hear ultimately that he was a "big *boy* / Doing a man's work, though a child at heart." I am not one who reads this poem as an indictment of child labor. That smacks of grievance, and Frost believed poems should be made of griefs, not grievances. I believe that the word *boy* is repeated so often and so deliberately to imbue with grief this catastrophic rite of passage: from boyhood to manhood to death at one stroke.

And Frost runs the range of repetition for effect, including Coleridge's acknowledgment of its necessity:

> the *apparent* tautologies of intense and turbulent feeling, in which the passion is greater and of longer endurance, than to be exhausted or satisfied by a single representation of the image or incident exciting it.

Surely we hear it in the boy's exhortation to his sister, "Don't let him cut my hand off— / The doctor, when he comes. Don't let him sister!" But there is also the repetition of "supper," first said as a welcome sign of the day's end: "His sister stood beside them in her apron / To tell them 'Supper.'" Then rendered fatally sinister when, "At the word, the saw, / As if to prove saws knew what supper meant, / Leaped out at the boy's hand, or seemed to leap." And the word "saw" itself undergoes a curious and telling transformation, from the accidental weapon that ends the boy's life, to the knowledge that enters the boy himself, from noun to verb: "the boy saw all."[3]

Hand is the other word most repeated: "the saw, / as if to prove saws knew what supper meant, / Leaped out at the boy's *hand*," "He must have given the *hand*," "But the *hand*!" "He swung toward them holding up the *hand*," "'Don't let him cut my *hand* off,'" "But the *hand* was gone already." When the boy has seen all spoiled, what has he seen? The maiming that will impair a life of manual labor. A diminishment of him as a man, a handicap as a human being, a kind of castration, and perhaps even the end of his life. "All" and the word is repeated, "all [is] spoiled." The repetition in the poem draws us close to the same sense of "allness," that unbearable state—the intolerable touch of poetry, Frost called it—that repetition is always hinting at.

Much has been made of the ending of "'Out, Out—'" with its ambiguous representation of the witnesses, who "Listened at his heart" as they heard, "Little—less—nothing!" Is it callousness that makes them turn away, once the boy, like a collapsed edifice or faulty foundation, offers no more to build on? Surely their affairs include whatever formal ones such a death entails, planning for his funeral and burial. But I want to consider the title, with its allusion to Macbeth. When he learns the news of his wife's death, Macbeth utters his famous speech:

> To-morrow, and to-morrow, and to-morrow,
> Creeps in this petty pace from day to day,

3. I want to thank Meghan O'Rourke for sharing this insight about the word *saw* as noun and verb in Frost's poem.

To the last syllable of recorded time;
And all our yesterdays have lighted fools
The way to dusty death. Out, out, brief candle.
Life's but a walking shadow; a poor player,
That struts and frets his hour upon the stage,
And then is heard no more: it is a tale
Told by an idiot, full of sound and fury,
Signifying nothing.

The speech he gives is nihilistic and desperate, the expression of one who has had enough of life's repetitions, and the allusion suggests that this boy's life in Frost's poem signifies no more than the lives Macbeth has himself snuffed out. But are we to take the comparison so far? The pattern of repetition in unfolding the story of a poem is my interest here. The title of Frost's poem, literally a fragment of Macbeth's speech, has an exclamatory resonance, like shouting, and echoes the boy's outcry, his rueful laugh when the saw meets his hand. The title mirrors the poem's construction, it shares the poem's pattern of repetition, and takes on Frost's, not Macbeth's, intended feeling for the events: the urgent desire to hold onto life, even as it is snatched away.

Andrew Hudgins's "Beatitudes," in the ancient form of Biblical anaphora and parallelism, gives us a perspective we have all experienced.

Blessed is the Eritrean child,
flies rooting at his eyes for moisture. Blessed
the remote control with which I flipped on past.
Blessed the flies whose thirst is satisfied.
Blessed the parents, too weak to brush way
the vibrant flies.
                    Blessed the camera crew
and blessed the gravity of Dan Rather, whose voice
grows stranger with every death he sees. Blessed

my silence and my wife's as we chewed our hot
three-cheese lasagna.
                    Blessed the comedies
we watched that night, the bed we slept in, the work
we rose to and completed before we sat
once more to supper before the television,
a day during which the one child died
and many like him. Blessed is the small check
we wrote and mailed. Blessed is our horror.

From *Ecstatic in the Poison* (2003)

"Habit is a great deadener," says Beckett. "Human kind cannot bear very much reality," says T. S. Eliot. And yet what do a couple who eat their dinner every night while watching the news on TV expect to see, except things that are sure to unsettle them? Here the challenge to the poet is to take the form of the Beatitudes past irony to the horror he concludes with, from the protective detachment that irony affords, to the overwhelming feeling which TV does indeed keep cool at a distance. The arc requires considering what the poem calls to be blessed, for the anaphora of beatitudes weighs each of the blessed equally, although if you recall the Sermon on the Mount, the rewards Jesus promises each of the blessed are not equal, e.g. those who mourn will be comforted, while the meek shall inherit the earth, and those persecuted for righteousness' sake will have the kingdom of heaven.

The role of irony in Hudgins's poem is to remind us that the blessing he wishes on the Eritrean child surely counts for more than the blessing on the remote control. Surely. Or does it? Everything he blesses plays a part in how one lives with the knowledge of a starving child, how one responds and turns to ones affairs, how one goes on living, thanks to the distracting and healthy repetitions of daily, middle class life, which affords us a small check to send to alleviate the suffering. It is a note of

Andrew Hudgins in particular that he would ask a blessing on the flies "whose thirst is satisfied" by the moisture in the child's eyes. But it is also the route by which he transcends irony. Those "vibrant flies" have as strong an urge to live as the child and its parents, stronger in fact. They are part of the horror, indeed, but they are also keeping themselves alive, every bit as much as the couple eating their "three-cheese lasagna." This is the risk Hudgins often runs in a poem, asking sympathy for life that might repel us, asking us as Robert Lowell did to "pity the monsters." They inspire us with horror, yet deserve our pity, even our blessing, especially when we recognize ourselves as one of them, feeding on the image produced by the camera crew and mediated by the newscaster. We end up filled with horror, at what the child is suffering, how we have been offered the image as an item of consumption, and how, repelled, we have turned to our affairs. The pattern of repetition in this poem tells the story of this complex feeling: that our horror is blessed, as is our consciousness of horror, and our ability to articulate our horror, our willingness to represent horror, to acknowledge it, and to tell its story in patterns and forms that make it stick in the minds of others as poetry.

That was where I ended when I first drafted this essay. But my family admonished me for concluding with some depressing poems. My weakness as a reader has always been a greater interest in how a thing is said than in what is said. So let me end with a poem by George Herbert which has a remarkably contemporary feel to it, a poem that performs some of the patterns of repetition I have been talking about, while existing as one of Coleridge's "apparent tautologies." It is a prayer about prayer, in which prayer itself is named repeatedly, each time with a difference.

Prayer (I)

Prayer the church's banquet, angel's age,
God's breath in man returning to his birth,

The soul in paraphrase, heart in pilgrimage,
The Christian plummet sounding heav'n and earth;

Engine against th' Almighty, sinner's tow'r,
Reversed thunder, Christ-side-piercing spear,
The six-days world transposing in an hour,
A kind of tune, which all things hear and fear;

Softness, and peace, and joy, and love, and bliss,
Exalted manna, gladness of the best,
Heaven in ordinary, man well drest,
The milky way, the bird of Paradise,

Church-bells beyond the stars heard, the soul's blood,
The land of spices; something understood.

Like the sonnet by John Donne, this one brings its built-in pattern, with a variation added by Herbert, an envelope-rhyme in the third quatrain of an otherwise English sonnet. But notice that any predicate, any verb that might complete a sentence for these nominative clauses, has been suppressed. Now each epithet tells a story. The rhythm in 10 of the 14 lines (1, 3, 5, 6, 7, 8, 10, 11, 12, and 14), where a caesura divides pairs of epithets, works against the iambic pentameter and recalls to my ear the rocking tetrameter of Anglo Saxon verse with its kennings: "Reversed thunder, Christ-side-piercing spear," "Heaven in ordinarie, man well drest," "Church-bels beyond the starres heard, the souls bloud."

This is an ancient rhythm and metaphorical mode for an ancient means of communication. Albeit in the seventeenth century, it is, to quote Frost, an old-fashioned way of being new. "Prayer" is a poem in which the lambent, imagistic, often non-linear, associative thinking of prayer itself is reflected, reproduced, repeated, in an apprehensible pattern. It is a poem at once elevated (prayer is "Exalted Manna, gladnesse of the best") and colloquial (it is also "A kinde of tune"). It is a poem without any of the devices of narrative or logical argument which yet manages to tell a story and make an argument thanks to metaphor and the sonnet form. Finally, having given prayer over two dozen names, including the list of abstractions in line nine, Herbert resolves on a strikingly modern indeterminate pronoun in remarkably plain language. Prayer is "something understood." He ends with the intimacy of the act, that aspect which is non-verbal and yet crucial. We pray for the same reasons we write poetry: to understand and be understood. And a poem, like a prayer, needs to be about something—something worth repeating.

American Devotions

In the English tradition, devotional poetry belongs to the first half of the seventeenth century. It reached whatever excellence it achieved in the sacred poems of John Donne and George Herbert. John Donne's "Holy Sonnets" and George Herbert's poems from *The Temple* treated religious matters having to do solely with Christian belief as a public, but primarily a personal, concern. The personal emphasis in both poets is crucial. Devotional worship, though it may be corporate or communal in practice, also connotes a private approach to God. John Donne addresses God in the 17th of his Holy Sonnets about a deeply private matter: the loss of his wife in childbirth. He strives to put her death in the context of orthodox belief.

> Since she whom I loved hath paid her last debt
> To Nature, and to hers, and my good is dead,
> And her soul early into heaven ravishèd,
> Wholly on heavenly things my mind is set.
> Here the admiring her my mind did whet
> To seek thee, God; so streams do show the head;
> But though I have found thee, and thou my thirst hast fed,
> A holy thirsty dropsy melts me yet.

But why should I beg more love, whenas thou
Dost woo my soul, for hers offering all thine:
And dost not only fear lest I allow
My Love to Saints and Angels, things divine,
But in thy tender jealousy dost doubt
Lest the world, flesh, yea, devil put thee out.

I think we can recognize the grief-stricken anxiety of the poem, even as we may be uncomfortable with the paradoxical resolution. Donne acknowledges God's jealous insistence that the love he offers to the bereft poet should be sufficient, and admits that this jealousy is "tender" and based on a divine doubt that the grieving widower can resist temptation. Still, the last six lines are inflected with a question ("But why should I?") which subtly suggests a lack of acceptance on Donne's part. It's hard to believe and to be a believer. Herbert can also sound like one of our contemporaries (and that is partly my point here), in his suspicion of the way grace is offered. Donne knows what he's lost, but fears he is not convinced that God's love can assuage his grief. In the following poem, Herbert thinks he's lost and can't quite believe what he's being offered. The action itself is as simple as one of Christ's parables. It's hard for Herbert, too, to believe that.

Love (III)

Love bade me welcome. Yet my soul drew back
    Guilty of dust and sin.
But quick-eyed Love, observing me grow slack
    From my first entrance in,
Drew nearer to me, sweetly questioning,
    If I lacked any thing.

A guest, I answered, worthy to be here:
    Love said, You shall be he.
I the unkind, ungrateful? Ah my dear,
    I cannot look on thee.

Love took my hand, and smiling did reply,
  Who made the eyes but I?

Truth Lord, but I have marred them: let my shame
  Go where it doth deserve.
And know you not, says Love, who bore the blame?
  My dear, then I will serve.
You must sit down, says Love, and taste my meat:
  So I did sit and eat.

Donne's poem sets a model of urgency for the contemporary devotional poem, but Herbert's is a model of ambiguity. Both are about the challenges of belief. There is no doubt that these are the kinds of poems we associate with devotional poetry. As poets and intellects, Donne and Herbert possessed gifts which made the form of their devotion one of the arts of poetry. Though the devotion may be practiced by anyone of faith, the art of the poet, especially a genius like Donne or Herbert, raises that practice to a level beyond most. It may be for this reason that Samuel Johnson cast doubt on writing poems as prayers, since he believed that the inventiveness of poetry undermines the sincerity of prayer, for prayer at its most personal and private may be inarticulate. T. S. Eliot addressed this notion in his 1935 essay "Religion and Literature." He argued that, at least from the modern point of view, devotional poetry as a form was destined for minor status. He actually assigns that rank to George Herbert in the same essay. Eliot might have dismissed John Donne as well if Donne had written only his religious poetry. Still, Eliot argues that the range of human interest in the devotional poem is narrow, and we know that Donne's range, in that regard, was greater than Herbert's. But wherever you come down on this argument—which I know may seem esoteric— for the devotional poem in English, Herbert and Donne set the benchmark. We can point to few poems for the next three centuries that rise to their level except Blake's *Songs of Inno-*

cence and *Songs of Experience* and the great eighteenth-century hymns. Still, Blake's poems are more like catechisms or Sunday school lessons than personal devotions. And the hymns are meant for group singing, corporate worship, and not as personal expression or for private meditation.

But also in the nineteenth century, Gerard Manley Hopkins wrote his extraordinary devotional poetry, known in its time principally to Robert Bridges, himself a poet and a writer, among other things, of Anglican hymns. Because I have an interest in devotional poetry, I place Hopkins in the same group with Donne and Herbert. I have looked for an example of his poetry which, like Donne's and Herbert's, gives a sense of the sound of the contemporary devotional poem. Here is a lesser known poem by Hopkins, in which by privately addressing himself and his soul, he may also be addressing God.

> My own heart let me more have pity on; let
> Me live to my sad self hereafter kind,
> Charitable; not live this tormented mind
> With this tormented mind tormenting yet.
>
> I cast for comfort I can no more get
> By groping round my comfortless, than blind
> Eyes in their dark can day or thirst can find
> Thirst's all-in-all in all a world of wet.
>
> Soul, self; come, poor Jackself, I do advise
> You, jaded, let be; call off thoughts awhile
> Elsewhere; leave comfort root-room; let joy size
>
> At God knows when to God knows what; whose smile
> 's not wrung, see you; unforeseen times rather—as skies
> Betweenpie mountains—lights a lovely mile.

As in the poems by Donne and Herbert, there is a strong sense of the interior conversation or monologue, and this interiority is an important feature of the poems I will be talking about.

I am also going to take up the address or apostrophe as an aspect of the devotional poem at any time, even when ambiguous. Nevertheless, that Eliot and others associate the devotional poem with another time or may consider it, in its limitations, minor doesn't seem to matter to those who have written devotional poetry—or what I am calling devotional poetry—in the twentieth century. Poets may continue to write devotional poetry because the possibilities of its subject have extended beyond conventional religious faith and, in American poetry, discovered in the best modern sense a tradition different from Donne's and Herbert's. Today I am talking about that new form of devotional poetry.

I'll begin with the most recent revival of the devotional poem as a practice of Christian worship. In "Eleven Addresses to the Lord" (from *Love & Fame*, 1970), John Berryman tried to write a devotional poem and, at the same time, to reawaken the form by making it new. Robert Lowell called Berryman's poem "one of the great poems of the age, a puzzle and a triumph to anyone who wants to write a personal devotional poem." He also noted the poem's "cunning skepticism." I think the skepticism which Lowell referred to is an essential element of any effective religious poem, at any time. In our time it has to be foremost and not simply present in that necessary element of any metaphor—irony. "Eleven Addresses to the Lord" is replete with frank statements of skepticism. Quatrains five and six of the first address provide a good example:

I have no idea whether we live again.
It doesn't seem likely
from either the scientific or the philosophical point of view
but certainly all things are possible to you,

and I believe as fixedly in the Resurrection-appearances to
    Peter & to Paul
as I believe I sit in this blue chair.

Only that may have been a special case
to establish their initiatory faith.

Berryman offers his skepticism, retracts it, then offers it again with qualifications. Without the skepticism the poem would be "merely" pious and not personal at all. It would certainly not be a poem that I would care to read. It would likely be, as Eliot noted in the aforementioned essay, "propaganda."

I can't avoid considering the religious import of Berryman's poem and its significance as he attempted to return to the Roman Catholicism of his youth, that "bright candle" of faith blown out by his father's suicide when he was twelve. I want to think about the poem in another way—as a way to write effective devotional poetry outside the boundaries of religious orthodoxy, in fact, outside the boundaries of religion altogether, a secular devotional poetry. Or let's say a quasi-secular devotional poetry. I will admit here, too, that the very term devotional suggests some devout attitude toward someone or something, like God, worthy of reverence and requiring a mode of address which recognizes a source of transcendent or ultimate meaning.

To quote Lowell again, Berryman's poem is an example of a personal devotional poem which suggests that there is a kind of "impersonal" devotional poem. Yet when I look back at the great English devotional poems of George Herbert and John Donne, they seem personal enough, especially Donne's Holy Sonnets with their urgent sense of apology and justification. In their poems Herbert and Donne are also working out orthodox theological arguments, adapting their own desires and anxieties to them. By personal I think Lowell means, and Berryman would agree, that though the poems address God, the God they imagine addressing is not one wholly defined by religious dogma. Berryman addresses a God of Rescue, as he calls him in a later poem:

You have come to my rescue again & again
in my impassable, sometimes despairing years.
You have allowed my brilliant friends to destroy themselves
and I am still here, severely damaged, but functioning.

This passage alone should cause us to acknowledge the personal, and that person is not as anxious as Herbert and Donne, or even Hopkins, to justify himself within a received form. The twisted, even devious syntax Berryman had perfected by the time he wrote the "Addresses" allows him in the second one to set himself apart from his fellow Christians and assert a personal belief:

I say 'Thy kingdom come,' it means nothing to me.
Has Thou prepared astonishments for man?
One sudden Coming? Many so believe.
So not, without knowing anything, do I.

Here, Berryman's address is Universalist in its acknowledgment of God's ubiquity and multiplicity. Addressing God as "Caretaker . . . Who haunt the avenues of Angkor Wat / recalling all that prayer, that glory dispersed," he asks God to "haunt me at the corner of Fifth & Hennepin," then adds three more epithets: "Shield & fresh fountain! Manifester! Even mine." Berryman uses a metaphorical name as the principal figure of speech in this poem. As soon as he brings God into the contemporary moment, he draws names again from the lexicon of the Bible. He wants to see God in a way that is fresh, yet part of a literary tradition:

I fell back in love with you, Father, for two reasons:
You were good to me, & a delicious author,
rational & passionate.

Then he adds, "Father Hopkins said the only true literary critic is Christ." That great unorthodox writer of sacred verses William Blake would have agreed and our poet himself declares, "Let me lie down exhausted, content with that."

Why did Lowell also regard the poem as a puzzle? I'm not sure. In *Love & Fame*, the book in which the poem appeared, Berryman departed from his famous "Dream Song" persona Henry, yet insisted that the poems of the book's title section, detailing his love life and literary celebrity, were not autobiographical. Did he mean that disclaimer to apply to "Eleven Addresses to the Lord" as well? The "Addresses" follow a series of boasting and gossipy revelations. But there are times when the boasting can still be heard, especially in the poet's claims of wretchedness and amazing grace:

> . . . Confusions & afflictions
> followed my days. Wives left me.
> Bankrupt I closed my doors. You pierced the roof
> twice & again. Finally you opened my eyes . . .
>
> Now, brooding thro' a history of the early Church,
> I identify with everybody, even the heresiarchs.

At times the poem reads like the poet's own twelve-step program—minus one. But Lowell saw it, and I am trying to see it, as a model for any one wanting to write a personal devotional poem. How can a puzzle be a model? And finally we know the poem did not rescue John Berryman from suicide, nor did the God of Rescue which it addresses.

Twice Berryman refers to widows in the "Addresses," once to his own: "Strengthen my widow." In the final section the poet imagines his end, contrasting it to the ends of early Christian martyrs, and speaks with some modesty while reminding us, not for the first time, of his career as a distinguished academic:

> Make too me acceptable at the end of time
> in my degree, which then Thou wilt award.

Cancer, senility, mania,
I pray I may be ready with my witness.

"Eleven Addresses to the Lord," like all devotional poems, is a poem of reverence, but if it is to succeed, it has to persuade us that the object of reverence has a living substance, even if that substance is of the imagination alone. I hope it goes without saying that we also have to be persuaded that the object is worthy of reverence. The God Berryman addresses is a personal God, and that deity's interest and care for individual human lives is assumed by faith, the substance of things unseen, and has been assumed for at least 4000 years. That is, Berryman didn't just make this God up for the sake of his poem, though some of the theological dimensions seem original with the poet.

Though Berryman's God is the "craftsman of the snowflake," and "sole watchman of the flying stars," still he addresses and imagines his God in abstract terms. "A Prayer for the Self" ends "Lift up / sober toward truth a scared self-estimate." And in section 9, the poet quotes "an old theologian" who has stated that "even to say You exist is misleading." Finally the poet asks this incomprehensible God to "Bear in mind me."

Possibly because Berryman's milieu is academic and the poet Maurice Manning's is agrarian, Manning's deity in his collection *Bucolics* is entirely concrete and in every way the God personified in nature, present in a poem like Keats's "To Autumn" and identified by James Merrill in *The Changing Light at Sandover* as the God B—Biology. Published in 2007, Manning's series, although it portrays God as everpresent, as immanent, still suggests the uncertainty that God, called "Boss," cares about the poet in a personal way. Much can be assumed about Boss's oversight and involvement in creation, except that. Insofar as the speaker fits in with natural cycles, then he enjoys the fruits of Providence. Manning's title *Bucolics* takes us to the Classical pre-Christian world, one for which Wordsworth expresses nostalgia in his famous sonnet, "The World Is Too Much with Us."

Manning's Boss is associated entirely with rural and agricultural matters, and the speaker in the poems sounds at times like
an industrious and curious farmer. I am going to assume the
speaker is the poet, and not a persona like Wendell Berry's Mad
Farmer. He may simply be someone who lives in the country.
An urban dweller might define "Boss" in another way entirely.

> boss of the grassy green
> boss of the silver puddle
> how happy is my lot
> to tend the green to catch
> the water when it rains
> to do the doing Boss

Though the title, *Bucolics*, recalls Virgil, the speaker often sounds
like the Psalmist David. Unlike the Psalmist, the poet seems to
have an ongoing beef with his relationship to Boss:

> it doesn't matter how
> I feel about it what I want
> from you is nothing Boss compared
> to what you want from me you want
> it all to always go your way

The poet reminds us that this relationship is like that of a hired
man to his boss. He admits, "I guess you've got a lot / of hands
though I'm just one / of many Boss." He can imagine Boss is
the blackbird laughing at him from a tree as he reaches to pick
a pawpaw or the tree frog on the trunk looking at him upside
down. He also claims to imagine an anthropomorphic figure: "I
believe you're baby faced / Boss a face as smooth as an onion,"
which nicely implies that like an onion Boss's identity is lay-
ered and may have nothing at heart. At times the poems sound
petulant, childish, and deliberately simple-minded, but never
for long.

that bare branch that branch made black
by the rain the silver raindrop
hanging from the black branch
Boss I like that black branch
I like that shiny raindrop Boss
tell me if I'm wrong but it makes
me think you're looking right
at me now isn't it a lark for me
to think you look that way
upside down like a tree frog
Boss I'm not surprised at all
I wouldn't doubt it for
a minute you're always up
to something I'll say one thing
you're all right all right you are
even when you're hanging Boss

The turn from the accidental to the intentional occurs so often that it appears to be the argument or aim of each of the seventy-eight poems in *Bucolics*. Although Boss seems to be regarding him from every facet of the natural world, he won't speak to the poet or give him a sign he doesn't have to guess at: "you know I never know for sure / I only know you bother me / from time to time you've caught my breath." When it comes to language, he admits, "your other favorite word / is not a word at all / you get so hushed up Boss / my ears get lonely I wish / you'd let me hear from you." This is a complaint of all believers. And like all of the poems, the range of the complaint runs from the simplest request to the most sophisticated. The second to last poem begins

am I your helper Boss or am
I not do I bring in the hay
for me or you or only for
the horse

The last poem ends: "O tell me why I can't hold back / this bitter thought are you the bee / or just the stinging story Boss." And there we are with the modern dilemma of religious belief. It may be beautiful and profound that we cannot tell the dancer from the dance. But if we cannot tell the creator from the creation, is the creator's role compromised, if not irrelevant? We cannot write the personal devotional poem except to a God we have to imagine into existence.

Theologically, *Bucolics* has more in common with "Eleven Addresses to the Lord" than either has to the next poem. But as a reverential address, Jean Valentine's "Lucy" is as much a devotional poem as Manning's or Berryman's. Valentine's poem, a sequence from her 2010 book *Break the Glass*, is addressed to the fossil skeleton discovered in Ethiopia in 1974, of a "southern ape of Afar" or "Australopithecus afarensis," a female believed at the time to be the oldest hominid ancestor of the human family. An epigraph to the sequence informs us that in Ethiopia people refer to her with a term that means "You are beautiful"— "Dinekenesh." Elements in the poem suggest ancestor worship, a reading the poet clearly invites. As a devotional poem "Lucy" brings much more to bear than that response. For Valentine, Lucy is not only a prime example of the feminine, but possibly of the poet. The poet's passionate address to this remarkable collection of fossilized human bones offers many interesting ways into the poem and to the sense of the personal devotion.

After the historical note about Lucy's identity (her name was given her by her discoverers who determined that despite her small brain she must have walked upright and must have been female), Valentine provides an address as introduction:

Lucy
your secret book
that you leaned over and wrote just in the dirt—

Not having to have an ending
Not having to last

For the poet, Lucy is not only an ancestral mother, but also possibly some kind of writer herself—one without any obligation to art and posterity but to the making of art; she may be the embodiment of poetry itself. The power with which Lucy is endowed by Valentine's imagination has been passed on to the poet. The dedicatory poem is followed by a quotation from Psalm 139, verse 16: "in thy book all my members were written, which in continuance were fashioned, when as yet there was none of them." This emphasizes Lucy's role as forebear, until we dwell on the notion that the worshiper's members "were written." But because the Psalm 139 is addressed to the Lord, as an epigraph the passage reminds us of Lucy's relationship to the poet. She is to the poet Jean Valentine what the Lord is to the Psalmist. It is partly this relationship which makes "Lucy" a devotional poem as I am defining it.

As such Lucy takes on several roles as the recipient of veneration. She is a blessed mother:

> I rush outdoors into the air you are
> Lucy
> and you rush out to receive me
> At last there you are
> who I always knew was there
> but almost died not
> meeting
> when my scraped-out child died Lucy
> you hold her, all the time

She is also a classical psychopomp, a guide of souls to the realm of the dead:

> Lucy, when Jane in her last clothes
> goes across   with Chekhov
> you are the ferryman

Lucy is like the angel in Jacob's wrestling match:

Still all night long my
Lucy I entreat you
I will not let thee go except thou bless me.

And finally she is that blending of act and intention which is
possible only in the presence of the muse:

How did you pray, Lucy?
You *were* prayer.
Your hands and toes.
When writing came back to me
I prayed with lipstick
on the windshield
as I drove.
Newton made up with the world,
he had already turned himself
into gold, he was already there.

Skeleton Woman,
in down
over around

I would like to say that Lucy is the poet's muse but I think she
represents something more, or perhaps she is simply another
way of thinking of the muse. Lucy is the poet's connection with
the very creation out of which she makes poetry:

Lucy
my saxifrage that splits the rocks
wildgood
mother
you fill my center-hole
with bliss
No one is so tender in her scream
Wants me so much

Not just, but brings me to be   Is
when I am close to death
and close to life.

Lucy is the rock-breaking flower of the William Carlos Wil-
liams poem which Valentine alludes to in this passage, and she
is also, as a fossil relic, the rock itself. For this flower, Valentine
has stated clearly, "I gave all I had to the poor . . ." On this rock,
she has built her poem.

The Lord God, Boss, Lucy—they are real presences, living substances, for which Berryman, Manning, and Valentine
have written poems of devotion. And yet I don't think this is
the whole story, for if the devotional form is going to endure
(and I think it will), then it must address the absence, the non-
existence, of any conventional deity which for over a century
now poetry has recognized. Even Berryman's Christian God
is a novel imagining of God, as are Manning's Boss and Valentine's Lucy. They are products of the imagination which the
poet insists or hopes will respond. Modern devotional poetry
intends to make up for that absence and non-existence with
subjects once worthy of holy reverence. But I want to speak now
of devotional poems which treat that absence itself as a living
substance.

The long poem, "Letters for the Dead," at the heart of Philip
Levine's 1933, which he published in 1973, is a sequence in ten
parts which purports to be what the title implies: written news
posted to those departed, in particular to the poet's father
whose death in 1933 when the poet was five gives the book's title
its significance. The fourth stanza of the first part speaks of trying "to say / something to each of you / of what it is / without
you." So the particularity of the father's death becomes gener-
alized and multiplied. What follows is a world so replete with
absences, so completely divorced from any sense of a transcendent being, any divinity to address, even a deceased parent, that
it may seem paradoxical to call the poem devotional. But scene

after scene, life after life, as it is depicted works iconically, as if each could be held up to the absent God to demonstrate "what it is / without you." Levine is famous for turning negations into affirmations, and that characteristic of his poetic style is no less present here. Since you are absent, the poem implies:

your briefcase
bulged with rusting tools

your shoes aged
the toes curling upward
in a spasm

your voice, your high voice
of pear and honey
shuddered once along the bare walls

but someone ate the pear
someone ate the honey
—we still ate at the usual hours

and went off to the factories in the dark
with bloodless sandwiches
folded in wax paper
with tiny packages of sweets

no one felt your sleep
arriving
or heard the sudden intakes of fear

no one held your hands
to keep them still
or your face glowing like a clock's

In the poem things spill their tears as they age, but the remembered voice has been consumed by death, and the living go on surviving in a familiar Levine landscape of exhausting factory work. There is also the alternative to this landscape, typical of

Levine as well, that of Spain with its pastoral life set against an even more tragic history than Detroit's. Yet even in Spain, the absence which Levine addresses, which informs his devotions, takes shape as a series of negations:

The sea calmed
the village darkened toward dawn
I was there

awake in a strange room
my children
breathing slowly in the warm air

down the hall
the workers bunched together
three to a bed grunting
in sleep

beside me my wife
in still another world

on the roof
not a single light

the sea reflecting
nothing
one black wave untipped
with spray
slipping toward shore
to spread like oil
—and then no more

nothing moved
no wind
no voice
no sound of anything
not one drop riding down my face
to scald the earth

In devotional poems (including those I have talked about so far), the poet is anxious to know his or her proper relationship to the one addressed, that lord and power, and to know what that lord and power might expect or require. It is as if the Lord or Boss or Lucy had set a series of spiritual tasks which the poet had to figure out and perform, one of which is, of course, to write the poem. This is not the case with Levine. He has set himself to say "what it is / without you." I interpret that as "How we live life without you. Write poetry. Love our families. Anticipate death—without you." That "you" is not only the poet's father but God. The poem tells what the essentials of living are like "without you." They can be exalted in their commonplace pleasure, nightmarish both awake and asleep, and mysterious in their consolations:

I ate an apple
the skin the sour white meat
the core
how I relished
the juice

Praise the apple

I struck my strange tall son
again and again
until my wife came begging
from our bed
and pulled me away

for 40 days
I dreamed my death like yours
at great speed
the bones shattering into meat
blood blurring the world
the spirit issuing outward
in a last breath

and came to land
weak and alive
the sunlight crossed my bed
I rose and fed the cat
the green worms fattened
on the vine
I looked in the corners
of things

Ultimately the dead are informed that their power dissipates as they are forgotten:

your books on the shelf
give up their words
one by one

your wedding band
with its secret calligraphy of wear
sleeps in a coffee can . . .

warm days—
the child you never saw
weeds the rhubarb
white grains collect above his lips
and flake away in the sudden wind

Neither Berryman's Lord, nor Manning's Boss, nor Valentine's Lucy is as circumscribed by time, as Levine's dead are, because none of them need to be remembered. Even Valentine's Lucy, as part of the fossil record, exists apart from time. But the non-being of the dead has its paradoxical existence only as long as the living who remember them. It is this information, useless really, which the letters of the poem convey. And so at the end of his poem Levine steps away from the mode of address, which keeps the poem personal in its anti-devotion, and steps back into the detached third person, stating in the last line: "even the dead are growing old."

Levine's devotional poem is in a sense an anti-devotion, bleak and bitter for the most part, and only indirectly acknowledges the power which precludes transcendence. That power is time. Berryman's God—his redeemer Christ—is unbounded by time and transcends it, allowing him to be present in the poet's life and to come to his rescue, albeit mysteriously. Levine believes in no such God. Yet "Letters for the Dead," as it shares the news of "what it is / without you," implies that the one enduring presence in the world of absences is time. Time circumscribes existence. There is no way beyond it. I believe the tone of anger running through Levine's poem has to do with the recognition of this fact. And though I risk inferring too much psychologically about the origin of Levine's poem, such an anger has to do with a loss of some former faith, like the loss of Levine's father. Berryman too speaks of the loss of his faith at his father's suicide. But "Eleven Addresses to the Lord" has to do with his recovery of faith, now with a more adult dimension.

Devotional poetry not only expresses faith in something or someone, like God or time, but gives us a sense that the poet is attempting to reconcile him or herself to the necessary reality of that object of reverence by establishing a personal, even private relationship with it. This is better demonstrated with examples, of course, which in poetry never entirely conform to an abstract definition. Over many years, Charles Wright has created a devotional style in the vein I am trying to describe. He recognizes that time is lord of the universe and of our lives. *Sestets*, his most recent book, offers us a form—a six line poem based implicitly on the part of the sonnet after the turn—that reflects the circumscription of time. After the octave or first eight lines of the sonnet, when the sestet begins we can feel the end coming. His attitude toward this inevitability, unlike Levine's, is as he says in the poem "Future Tense," "bittersweet."

All things in the end are bittersweet—
An empty gaze, a little way station just beyond silence.

If you can't delight in the everyday,
            you have no future here.
And if you can, no future either.

And time, black dog, will sniff you out,
            and lick your lean cheeks,
And lie down beside you—warm, real close—and will not
   move.

This is not to say that Wright eschews any sense that time might
be transcended and a connection with a transcendent reality
achieved. His poetry has become capacious enough to allow for
the feeling, if not the fact, to be embodied. The titles of these
sestets often read like first lines. "The Evening Is Tranquil, and
Dawn Is a Thousand Miles Away":

The mares go down for their evening feed
            into the meadow grass.
Two pine trees sway the invisible wind—
            some sway, some don't sway.
The heart of the world lies open, leached and ticking with
   sunlight
For just a minute or so.
The mares have their heads on the ground,
            the trees have their heads on the blue sky.
Two ravens circle and twist.
            On the borders of heaven, the river flows clear a bit longer.

The very first poem in *Sestets* lets us know where we are going
in an existence determined and circumscribed by time. "Tomorrow":

The metaphysics of the quotidian was what he was after:
A little dew on the sunrise grass,

A drop of blood in the evening trees,
        a drop of fire.

If you don't shine you are darkness.
The future is merciless,
        everyone's name is inscribed
On the flyfleaf of the Book of Snow.

In describing the poems by Berryman, Manning, Valentine, and even Levine, I have said that an element of their devotional nature is that they address objects worthy of devotion. In many of his *Sestets* Wright is talking to himself, as do so many modern lyric poets. But "Tomorrow" also suggests in the turn from third person to second person that he is speaking to the reader and that implies another sort of faith—faith that a reader exists. Here is the greatest expression I know of that faith, the last section of "Song of Myself":

The spotted hawk swoops by and accuses me, he complains of
    my gab and my loitering.

I too am not a bit tamed, I too am untranslatable,
I sound my barbaric yawp over the roofs of the world.

The last scud of day holds back for me,
It flings my likeness after the rest and true as any on the
    shadow'd wilds,
It coaxes me to the vapor and the dusk.

I depart as air, I shake my white locks at the runaway sun,
I effuse my flesh in eddies, and drift it in lacy jags.

I bequeath myself to the dirt to grow from the grass I love,
If you want me again look for me under your boot-soles.

You will hardly know who I am or what I mean,
But I shall be good health to you nevertheless,
And filter and fibre your blood.

Failing to fetch me at first keep encouraged,
Missing me one place search another,
I stop somewhere waiting for you.

Of course, we all know that Walt is celebrating himself, that container of multitudes who finds it as lucky to die as to be alive. But if devotional poems as part of their nature have to express faith in something, faith is after all the substance of things hoped for and the evidence of things unseen. In this case, you and me. Whitman's faith, in this greatest of American devotional poems, is that there will be a reader who will find him. I think he shares this faith with all poets, even those who profess to have no faith at all.

I have made many assumptions in trying to extend the definition of devotional poetry beyond a religious tradition. These assumptions, however, are based obviously on my own Christianity and the way it has informed my thinking. But I have also been guided for years by a late poem by Emily Dickinson:

1551

Those—dying then,
Knew where they went—
They went to God's Right Hand—
That Hand is amputated now
And God cannot be found—

The abdication of Belief
Makes the Behavior small—
Better an ignis fatuus
Than no illume at all—

That will-o'-the wisp or foolish fire, the ignis fatuus, is a powerful guide, as Emily Dickinson modestly suggests, since it produces larger behavior than not believing at all. The devotional poem, in any form, is the opposite of an abdication of belief. It is an affirmation.

In this discussion of craft, I have emphasized craft's thematic dimension. I have loosely used the term *form,* especially since the poems I have referred to vary in their formal construction, though even Berryman's depart from the recognizable English verse tradition, which underlies much of what we call formal poetry today. John Crowe Ransom describes the notion of form I have in mind in his essay "Forms and Citizens":

> By formal we are not to mean the metre only; but also, and it is probably even more important, the literary type, with its fictitious point of view from which the poet approaches his object, and its prescription of style and tone. And by tradition we should mean simply the source from which the form most easily comes. Tradition is the handing down of a thing by society, and the thing handed down is just a formula, a form. (*The World's Body*, 1938)

I have ended with poems by Whitman and Dickinson, however, because they exemplify Ransom's first sense of what tradition is, "the source from which the form most easily comes." Whether intentionally or not, the poets I have talked about here have discovered a tradition or source for their devotional poetry which is different from George Herbert's and John Donne's and all who attempt to address the God of Christianity in verse. I am aware that this tradition is alive in English poetry, at least in the work of Geoffrey Hill. But I would argue that even John Berryman among the five poets I have talked about finds his source in Whitman and Dickinson. The tradition of the American devotional poem—radical in imagination and heterodox in belief—begins with them.

Writing as a Daily Practice

P rayer is a waking activity, a way of giving thanks for consciousness. We may pray subconsciously, we may pray in
our dreams. These are moot points, even mute points. When
prayer takes the form of devotion, and devotion takes the form
of poetry, the connection is through consciousness. If writing
a poem is an act of devotion, and devotion is a form of prayer,
then being awake is most often the condition in which devotion, prayer, and writing poetry most readily take place. We
may compose poems subconsciously (in fact, I believe we do),
we may compose poems in our dreams. But to speak of a devotional life as a daily one implies being awake, being conscious,
deliberately engaged in the activity of prayer. Devotions are
often personal. The connection with the personal and private
activity of writing poetry seems to me obvious, especially if one
writes daily—or nightly—and believes the activity of writing
a poem is a form of communication with God, that is, a deliberate and conscious attempt to unite oneself through language
with our Creator. Devotional poetry, then, as a form of prayer,
enacted in putting words into verse on a page (or a screen), or
simply into memory, gives thanks for the consciousness which
makes it possible. But it also gives thanks for the regular activity and practice which can be called daily.

The acknowledgment of devotional poetry is articulated in a number of ways, especially in the works of W. H. Auden and John Berryman who have based sequences of poems on the canonical hours, those markers of daily devotion that stretch back to ancient Judaism. I wish I could say I had attempted something like Auden's "Horae Canonicae," a poem that marks each of the holy hours of the original Friday—the Good Friday—of Christ's crucifixion and follows the flawed human beings who participated in that crime without knowing what they did. I have written about prayer in my original sequence of "Unholy Sonnets," twenty of which appeared in my book *Questions for Ecclesiastes*, and others in other books.

A word about the title "Unholy Sonnets." I originally wrote these in response to John Donne's "Holy Sonnets." My project didn't last long once I recognized that Donne was a Jacobean genius in fear for his mortal soul, and I was simply a modern American Christian who wanted to explore his belief, though with no less fearfulness. I gave my poems the apparently sacrilegious title "Unholy Sonnets" in order both to ward off piety and to invite readers in who might not believe as I do; to surprise them with a devotional poem. Once the poems started appearing in print, twenty-five years ago, a fellow poet said, "I don't know, Mark, they seem pretty holy to me."

But the poem as prayer and the prayer as poem seems to be a habit of writing of mine since I first began writing. These poems betoken both a daily practice of communication with God and a daily practice of writing itself. They record the activity of prayer in some diurnal situation, as in church, for example, or as the following one records, falling asleep.

11

Half asleep in prayer I said the right thing
And felt a sudden pleasure come into
The room or my own body. In the dark,
Charged with a change of atmosphere, at first

I couldn't tell my body from the room.
And I was wide awake, full of this feeling,
Alert as though I'd heard a doorknob twist,
A drawer pulled, and instead of terror knew
The intrusion of an overwhelming joy.
I had said thanks and this was the response.
But how I said it or what I said it for
I still cannot recall and I have tried
All sorts of ways all hours of the night.
Once was enough to be dissatisfied.

Writing daily, like praying daily, may involve a certain amount of improvisation. The great eighteenth-century poet and critic Samuel Johnson suspected the innovation of poetry as a means of praying, which he believed was subliterate, even inarticulate, in order to be sincere. Still, as a form of meditation, the construction of a sonnet is the kind of blending of writing and praying that I am talking about. That "eye on the object look" Auden speaks of in his "Horae Canonicae" that the person dedicated to a task shows, as he or she becomes one with the endeavor. In writing a poem we can lose ourselves in the process, just as we may do in praying. But one of the things I never want to do is to prescribe my way of working to my students, nor would I want to prescribe my way of praying.

The power of corporate or public prayer is not lost on me, though I'm talking here about the privacy of personal devotions. Still, most liturgies I know of combine corporate and private prayer during a church service, and the way the church year unfolds not only from Sunday to Sunday, but in daily forms like the lectionary—the readings of Scripture—reminds us that the formal practice of worship is a daily one. I have one poem which contrasts the power of congregational worship and corporate prayer with the unspoken secret preoccupation which may not have been relieved or answered in the act of public confession. The occasion of this poem remains vivid to me. I teach in a university in which there is a good deal of hierarchy, i.e. Chancellor—Provost—Dean—Chair—Faculty. And many years ago a Dean was trying to deny me something I thought I deserved. It doesn't matter now, but I remember that the poisonous resentment I had stored within myself made my attendance at church one Sunday an important reckoning: I wanted to be cleansed of a feeling I knew was a sin.

14

After the praying, after the hymn-singing,
After the sermon's trenchant commentary
On the world's ills, which make ours secondary,
After communion, after the hand-wringing,
And after peace descends upon us, bringing
Our eyes up to regard the sanctuary
And how the light swords through it, and how, scary
In their sheer numbers, motes of dust ride, clinging—
There is, as doctors say about some pain,
Discomfort knowing that despite your prayers,
Your listening and rejoicing, your small part
In this communal stab at coming clean,
There is one stubborn remnant of your cares
Intact. There is still murder in your heart.

This poem is an Italian sonnet, that is, it combines a section of eight lines, rhyming ABBAABBA with one of six lines rhyming CDECDE. Not all the rhymes are as exact as they might be; "pain / clean" is inexact, for example. But as I constructed the sonnet I sensed what I was working toward, the incorrigible and sinful feeling that remained in my heart at the end of the church service which I had hoped would relieve me, purge me. Setting that up, as I do at the end of the sonnet, really caused me to examine the feeling itself, the "stubborn remnant" of what I call my "cares," though even that word mitigates the actual criminal feeling I had at heart. I knew there would be a sense of irony, even grim humor, if I could bring off the final enjambment and the clear, exact rhyme between "part" and "heart." Once I did, once I felt the poem close shut like a door, I really did feel as if I had separated, even expelled, the awful feeling from my soul. The poem itself became a confession. At the same time I had made a credible Italian sonnet which described the liturgy or order of worship in a Christian church on Sunday.

When I was of the age to start interrogating my parents about their private lives and still young enough to be puzzled by answers like "It's none of your business," I asked my mother when she prayed. She told me that she prayed in the morning, when she was washing the breakfast dishes, after everyone had left for the day. In a sequence of poems called "The Past from the Air," which is partly about the slow collapse of my parents' marriage and my mother's health, I tried to capture that moment, a daily one. I failed to note in the poem that my mother also worked, and clearly stole this time for herself before she had to leave for the day.

Praying

A wedge of morning sunshine bathes her hands.
The suds mount breeding like a hive of foam.
A bowl laden with floating steam descends
Into the underwater catacomb
Of crockery and silver, where the wands
Of fingers do their work. The plates become
Immaculate as halos. Then, the rack
Receives them; dried, they're piled into a stack.

She's praying as she does this, as she soaks
A sponge with liquid soap and looks outside,
Handling the chore, scrubbing the hardened yolks
And coffee stains, as if preoccupied
With one cloud breaking sunlight into spokes.
She's praying though her eyes are open wide.

She's doing three things, watching a cloud pass,
Talking to God, drying a drinking glass.

It is a perfect time to be alone
And easier, alone, to pray for those
Who've left her with the silent chaperone
Of the sun, watching through the kitchen windows,
Making the noise of work an undertone.
The image of her loved ones forms and grows
Like foam riddled with light. She holds it still,
A solid thing, for God to gaze his fill.

And what God sees, if God sees anything,
Looks like the crawling colors on a bubble
Before it breaks and drops a filmy rain
On someone's palm. He sees the vivid scrawl
Of light across creation, but no sign
Of prayer, which is abstract, invisible.
He sees a woman asking him to read
Her mind. He pities her. He cannot read.

I will admit that the God in this poem is more like the poet watching his mother than like God, but I wanted to foreshadow the fear my mother would at times embrace that she had not simply been left alone but abandoned by everyone, including God.

In a sense my poem "Praying" is a study of one person praying, a kind of ekphrasis. The meditation on an event in the life of Christ or one of his disciples can also be a basis for devotion, including devotional poetry. (In fact, St. Ignatius of Loyola, the sixteenth-century founder of the Jesuits, developed an entire set of spiritual exercises based on imagining for oneself the experiences of Jesus Christ.) I realized putting together this talk that ekphrastic poems meditating on works of art with religious subjects run through my work. The following poem while it compares two representations of the repentant Peter, after he has denied knowing Christ, focuses on the attitude of prayer, the way of praying, and the possibility that the answer to the prayer is always at hand and possibly involved in the act of praying itself.

Goya's *Saint Peter Repentant*

A little hilltop stepped on by a glacier—that's how he looks, his bald head nearly flat,
And the upward turning dog's eyes humble as heather, and the tufts of eyebrow and beard sheepish.
He's draped with orange clay and a curving seam of granite— his clothes.
I've never seen thicker hands in a painting of a saint. I've seen hands like them
On men who showed me how to do work that would wilt me by lunch hour, making me understand,
Later, why roofers spend half their lunch hour lying in shade, if there is any, one arm flung over their eyes.
He looks sorry. He already has the keys, and yet he's sorry. Asking forgiveness is hard work.

Compare El Greco's Peter doing the same thing. Everything lengthens heavenward.
Beautiful, yes, and saintly, yes, but not Peter. Of all the apostles—the earthiest, the most creaturely.
He said one thing that pleased Jesus, though it pleased him mightily, and others that disappointed them both.
In Goya's painting, the keys to heaven lie on a stone like a mattress corner, their loops lapped by a fold of Peter's robe,
As if Peter, not yet a saint, didn't see them, or had put them aside until he finished his work.

At this point I should acknowledge that not all of what we call devotional poetry delights in consciousness or gives thanks for it as a condition which makes it possible to access the ear of God, to paraphrase George Herbert. I hear the darkest of Gerard Manley Hopkins's sonnets as a kind of reproach to my argument:

"I wake and feel the fell of dark, not day"

I wake and feel the fell of dark, not day.
What hours, O what black hours we have spent
This night! what sights you, heart, saw; ways you went!
And more must, in yet longer light's delay.
    With witness I speak this. But where I say
Hours I mean years, mean life. And my lament
Is cries countless, cries like dead letters sent
To dearest him that lives alas! away.

    I am gall, I am heartburn. God's most deep decree
Bitter would have me taste: my taste was me;
Bones built in me, flesh filled, blood brimmed the curse.
    Selfyeast of spirit a dull dough sours. I see
The lost are like this, and their scourge to be
As I am mine, their sweating selves; but worse.

As Hopkins expresses his dilemma, a sense of being lost and separate from God, a condition he recognizes when he wakes or comes to consciousness, Hopkins also recognizes that his letters, dead though they may be, still have been composed by a poet awake to his devotions. Though he feels these devotions are fruitless, because he himself is totally absorbed by his unworthiness, this sonnet is still a devotional poem and even its nocturnal occasion is a sign of its place in some daily order.

To exercise the power of prayer on one's own behalf is one thing; to exercise it on behalf of another is of course something I imagine all of us have done. Some years ago, while I was out of country, I learned that one of my children was undergoing a psychological crisis, one in which consciousness had ceased to feel like a gift. All I could do at the time was pray for her, but I could do one more thing, too. I could write her a poem, make an appeal for her well-being by creating that wrinkle in time and space which a poem is, bringing God to bear as God is always prepared to be. "To a Brainy Child in Distress":

Dear mind, suffering far away,
I am writing to you on the other side of the earth.

Belovèd thinker, dwelling on no thought
But pain and the pain of thinking, of the mind,

My mind is on you now. My thoughts,
Lit by a dawn you will not see for hours,

Are with you in your darkness, far away.
I hope it is the darkness of deep sleep,

Dear mind. Belovèd thinker, I hope you wake
Far from estranging trouble, home again

To a good thought, a changed mind.

Sometimes, often, in writing my poems, I feel obliged to explain Christians to non-Christians (in fact, that's what I'm doing most of the time). In the following poem, I return to my mother in her kitchen, while remembering a custom of the church where I grew up. The poem is called "The Prayer Chain." Some of you may even be familiar with something similar:

Mother's on the telephone, forging a link
In the prayer chain, a tub of suds
And dishes steaming in the sun-white sink.
And I wonder if the twisted phone cord

Is part of it. But she explains
That someone in the church is ailing.
And she calls to start a chain
Of prayers. She tells me this with feeling.

A cloud has dimmed the kitchen. Her face
Hardens with conviction. Once the chain
Is forged the call will come back to our place,
The closing link, the praying done.

This is circa 1961,
Redondo Beach, South Bay Christian Church.
I wonder if there's still such a thing
To pull the suffering into the reach—

Of what? Those links in the prayer chain?
For wasn't it the casting of
A spell, the binding of a span
Of power? They would have called it Love,

Believers with this one sense of magic,
Stringing the gold of faith from voice
To voice. Like Rimbaud. Or like Blake,
Beholding the dread tyger in its throes.

But that's not what they thought, surely,
Or what she thought. And yet the chain
Reached from earth to heaven, really,
Like the chain Milton imagined

Dangling planet earth like a bauble.
Their chain reached to a husband's
Cancer, a widow's broken hip, and hauled
Forth out of the depths, hand over hand,

The out-of-reach dying, the fallen-
And falling-to-pieces. You might shrug
At this quaint belief and its presumption,
Unless you'd felt, as they each had, its tug.

The literary allusions to Rimbaud, Blake, and Milton may
seem a bit pedantic, or a lot pedantic, but that's the world I live

in. I not only teach creative writing in a university, but I teach classes in literature. It's part of the way I think, and in this case I'm reminding people like myself that this "quaint belief" in a supernatural power can be found in parallel ways among some great poets.

At the beginning of the Holy Eucharist, Rite Two, of the Book of Common Prayer, the Priest who is celebrating the Eucharist says: Almighty God, to you all hearts are open, all desires known, and from you no secrets are hid: Cleanse the thoughts of our hearts by the inspiration of your Holy Spirit, that we may perfectly love you, and worthily magnify your holy Name; through Christ our Lord. *Amen.* The congregation joins in that *Amen.* It is one of the corporate prayers I find most moving as it asks God for the most intimate and private of interventions, an action that we have faith can be performed. One of my poems is an attempt to consider literally how God, in a transcendent act, may enter our mundane, earthbound lives. It is the very thing I think is aspired to in devotional poetry—a response from God to our daily life.

9

Almighty God, to you all hearts are open,
All throats, all voice boxes, all inner ears,
All pupils, all tear ducts, all cavities
Inside the skull inside the trick of flesh.
To you the face is like a picture window,
The body is a door of molded glass,
All lengths of gut are pasture, all membrane
Peels back and off like ripe persimmon skin.
And every wrinkle folded in the brain
Runs smoothly through your fingers and snaps back
Into its convolution. Even the blood
Is naked as a bolt of oilcloth.
You touch the working parts and track the thought,
A comet on your fingertip, and squint.

These few comments are in no way meant to be anything more than tentative. The truth is I don't know exactly what determines the dailiness of devotional verse, except that it seems to happen daily or nightly and records that fact frequently in its expression. I'm not even sure that devotional verse can be strictly defined within a religious context, especially when I think of it in the context of Walt Whitman's poetry, even Emily Dickinson's. I do know that what we call devotional poetry carries with it an implicit or explicit appeal to some power greater than the poet. For some reason the poet's devotion itself is often the issue. And it is this tension—frequently a dramatic one—to which readers who do not necessarily share the poet's beliefs are drawn. Why that is remains mystifying to me, as a believer, but not as a poet and a lover of poetry.

Dailiness

The first seven days: light, day, and night on day one; the
sky on day 2; earth and seas, plants and trees on day 3; on
day 4, stars, sun, moon; on day 5, land and sea animals, birds;
humankind, male and female, on day 6; on day 7, the Sewanee
Writers' Conference.

I am going to talk about dailiness, diurnal and nocturnal, and
what we do with the twenty-four hours of a day if we're writers.
Most of what I'll be talking about is writing poetry, a little bit as
Andrew Hudgins does in his essay, "Diary of a Poem," but I also
have in mind Richard Bausch's "Letter to a Young Writer," in
which Bausch quotes Flaubert saying, "Be regular and ordinary
in your habits, like a petty bourgeois, so you may be violent and
original in your work." When I think of dailiness it is not the
commonplace, but yes it is the commonplace, not the ordinary,
but yes it is the ordinary. I mean the days of creation, the time it
takes to make a thing—a poem is what I mainly mean, but since
it is a made thing I mean anything a writer works at daily to
complete. Dailiness is being at the desk daily, seeing it through.

It is like practicing, if you are a musician. I live with a musician, and I know or have witnessed that daily discipline, the scales, the vocalizing, the learning of new songs and process of memorization, the rehearsal of old songs and the refreshing of memory. The hours in the practice room, focused and self-directed.

In truth I've learned not to care how long it takes to write a poem. And I do think Yeats is right about a line that takes hours to write having to seem like a moment's thought. Although if you remember he said "maybe" it took hours.

> I said: 'A line will take us hours maybe;
> Yet if it does not seem a moment's thought,
> Our stitching and unstitching has been naught.
>> W. B. Yeats, "Adam's Curse"

I am aware that there are lines, whole poems, which come as gifts, apparently. But usually it takes a long time. Most of my poems take a long time to write, and I do measure that composition in days, sometimes, since I write in a notebook that does multiple duties, as diary, journal, drafting table, all usually run together. Still since I date each entry when I begin writing in the morning, I know the date a poem might begin. But when I make the transition to typing a draft, I can lose track. Sometimes I add the date when I think I have reached a final draft. But I've learned to be superstitious about that. Once I put the final date on a poem, I know it may be only wishful thinking.

One thing that I know will hinder me or make the process slow is having to admit to myself that a line I think is inspired—often one of the first lines I've written, as I'll show you later—has to go. The poem has reached a place where that line, which may have gotten the whole thing going, just doesn't belong anymore. It might do for another poem but it no longer fits with the one it has germinated. Admitting as much to myself includes a kind of self-analysis. I usually read early drafts aloud to my wife, and Amy will catch the problem, and I will respond with spirited resistance. But every day subsequently, day after day, slowly it dawns on me that the line has to go. And there's the hitch, it takes a long time sometimes *to let it* dawn on me, to admit that little darling needs another home or to be put out of its misery. (I just wrote "put out of its mystery" there. Maybe I should keep that.) So the stages of composition for me look something like this:

1. Draft with inspired line
2. Revision, even inspired revision
3. Dawning apprehension of disaster
4. Slow disintegration of inspired revision
5. Disaster
6. Rubble
7. New sense of commitment to rebuilding
8. Long slog accepted
9. Daily return to drafts, inspired and uninspired

But a day does come or usually does come when I see that a poem is finished. This can be a joyful occasion of thinking *Yes, the world must know!* or one of resignation, *Well, at least nobody has to see this.* I do keep a folder of incomplete drafts that I look at daily, and sometimes there's one that I've made daily progress on and it excites me to get to it. I will think I've finished a poem, go on with the other work I have to do (teaching, reviewing, writing an essay or craft lecture like this, shopping for dinner, cooking), and at the end of the day understand that the poem is all wrong, out of whack, and will need to be completely redone the next day. This is often a good sign. I look at the draft the next day and see that it does have something if I will only get rid of my favorite line!

How many days will pass? Though I date what I think of as the final draft, I keep undated typed copies of the drafts leading to it and have been doing this for maybe thirty years now. I tell myself that I don't care how long it took me to get to the end. I don't say anything about how long it took me to write which to me can sound both self-pitying and boastful. As the late Harris Wittels once said, this is humble bragging, as if to think that if a poem took you a long time and a lot of hard work, it must be worthy of praise. Readers of poetry don't care how long it took you to write the poem.

As for revision itself, it seems at times, in fact, just about always seems, that my writing is all revision. As a teacher I demand revision from my creative writing students, but I don't tell them how to write, except in a forms class, where I do give assignments: a ballad, a sonnet, blank verse, and so on. I don't tend to give prompts for subject or theme, unless asked by my students, and I usually don't give them to myself, except sometimes. That is, I don't recommend specific tools to students or even times of day (I feel as if I'm revising even now), but I do recommend that they make writing a habit. And even so, I don't require myself to begin something new every day, only to look every day at what I've done until I can let it go. Also I know I can let it go when it becomes more or less fixed in my memory and I can take pleasure saying it to myself aloud. This seems to be an advantage of writing poetry. A poem can go along with you, it is a mental traveler. There have been countless times when I have understood what I needed to do with a poem as I have been doing something else, like driving to work. Reciting the poem daily as I drive to work might lead to more revisions, but after a period of this, the poem leaves my memory. It passes into another room or grows up and leaves home and no longer requires attention all of the time. It's the end of that period that a sculptor I know, Richard Deutsch, calls "living in a dream." Then I start looking forward to the next spell or bewitchment and that may not come for months. Meanwhile there is the daily attention to drafts, the arising almost unbidden of some new notion, a phrase, say, from a list of ideas, most often memories. I have heard the poet Rosanna Warren refer to one notebook she has as her compost heap, and we know Yeats called his "the foul rag and bone shop of the heart." Thinking of my notebook and file of drafts in such highly enriched metaphorical language is inviting but also tends to put a romantic gloss on their banality. I don't want to dramatize my own writing process; poets are not heroes for doing what comes naturally, any more than saints are, but perhaps it's necessary to dramatize a little. I also recall once a poet displaying the multiple notebooks he kept with him, all beautiful products of Florentine stationers. As he showed them off I could see my students in the audience making notes about them. Later in class I said, "Don't think you have to spend a fortune on a Florentine blank book for your writing." But then I had violated a long held policy of not telling my students how they should do their work. If they want to drop seventy-five Euros on an exquisitely bound book at Il Papiro, why not? My own fetish is for cheap spiral notebooks and expensive pens.

If going to your notebook bound in gorgeous marbled paper will help you make writing a habit, so be it. You have to have the habit or what Seamus Heaney called "a work lust." Actually, that "work lust" is the advice Heaney's persona as pilgrim receives from James Joyce as shade in Heaney's poem "Station Island." I'll quote the passage since it's one that's haunted me ever since I read it years ago. The pilgrim, our protagonist, is visiting a holy island on a lough in Ireland and there encounters a number of ghosts, including the ghost of James Joyce who says, among other things,

"Your obligation
is not discharged by any common rite.
What you must do must be done on your own

so get back in harness. The main thing is to write
for the joy of it. Cultivate a work-lust
that imagines its haven like your hands at night

dreaming the sun in the sunspot of a breast."

If only one could "cultivate a work-lust" like an erotic drive. Of course, Freud saw the relationship between eros, which W. H. Auden called in his elegy for Freud "builder of cities," and labor.

But the way there, and there always seems to be a way there, requires perseverance, doesn't it, and curiosity and impulse, possibly a sense of how you are being called, if you are being called, if calling is even the word for it. Here's Muriel Rukeyser's "Then I Saw What the Calling Was."

> All the voices of the wood called "Muriel!"
> but it was soon solved;   it was nothing, it was not for me.
> The words were a little like Mortal and More and Endure
> and a word like Real, a sound like Health or Hell.
> Then I saw what the calling was   :   it was the road I traveled,
>   the clear
> time and these colors of orchards, gold behind gold and the full
> shadow behind each tree and behind each slope.   Not to me
> the calling, but to anyone, and at last I saw   :   where
> the road lay through sunlight and many voices and the marvel
> orchards, not for me, not for me, not for me.
> I came into my clear being;   uncalled, alive, and sure.
> Nothing was speaking to me, but I offered and all was well.
>
> And then I arrived at the powerful green hill.

I believe this poem can be read as Rukeyser's awakening to her own sexuality, her "clear being," her queerness. I don't think that precludes my reading of it as an allegory of the writing life, and the attraction, the erotic attraction, that draws us, moves us from the familiar to the strange, even our own strangeness if you will, and to discovery. Although Muriel hears her name called, then recognizes that the call isn't for her specifically, still she offers herself, "uncalled, alive, and sure." And she arrives at an important destination. Mark Strand has an essay in which he claims all such references to hills and mountains in poems are to Mount Parnassus, the classical home of the Muses. To me that "powerful green hill" is the discovery of an imminent and sometimes overwhelming commitment, a lifetime's dedication.

Randall Jarrell creates another sort of metaphor for daily persistence in his poem "Well Water." It is this poem that got me thinking about a writer's regular and ordinary practice.

What a girl called "the dailiness of life"
(Adding an errand to your errand. Saying,
"Since you're up . . ." Making you a means to
A means to a means to) is well water
Pumped from an old well at the bottom of the world.
The pump you pump the water from is rusty
And hard to move and absurd, a squirrel-wheel
A sick squirrel turns slowly, through the sunny
Inexorable hours. And yet sometimes
The wheel turns of its own weight, the rusty
Pump pumps over your sweating face the clear
Water, cold, so cold! you cup your hands
And gulp from them the dailiness of life.

That old fashioned pump, rusty, "hard to move and absurd," moving slowly "through the sunny / Inexorable hours" can stand in for the work habit, that primitive and backward procedure also described implicitly by Elizabeth Bishop in her late poem "12 O'Clock News," as "one of the most backward left in the world today." That is, writing. And those hours, which are relentless and will not yield to any plea while they pass, we know what they are. But as the poet says sometimes the wheel turns of its own weight, without our effort it seems, and the deliciously cold water "pumps over your sweating face." And this ordinary action yields that ordinary need—water, most delicious when you are hot and thirsty, while still representing and embodying the dailiness of life. W. H. Auden's take on that essence comes in his late poem in praise of rain, "First Things First": "Thousands have lived without love, not one without water." There is more than one poet who has made the claim that poetry is an essential element for life like water or love. It certainly is for the poet. And yet without loving that labor throughout the inexorable hours we will not only miss the water, but miss the occasion when it seems to have sprung unbidden from a profound source to fill a vital need.

Sometimes you lose track of time, dissolved in the activity of writing as if in prayer, undistracted, doing what you do, experiencing the joy of it, living in a dream, and recognizing only later that this work itself is the fulfillment of the work-lust.

That experience of working daily and intensely on a poem and knowing it's proving recalcitrant, yet knowing that it's worth doing, even for the sake of your own stubbornness is also what I'm talking about. And for all kinds of reasons. One is thinking that the poem has a life of its own, as I have suggested in "proving recalcitrant." But your own unconscious can work against you and your consciousness can work too hard. Or you can lack the ability. Usually when some breakthrough does occur, if you're alert, you may receive a gift from the same source as your breakthrough. Robert Frost told his biographer, Lawrance Thompson, about working all of a summer night on a draft of "New Hampshire," the title poem of his fourth book. "New Hampshire," not a great poem by any means, was very important to Frost as an attempt to define himself in a new direction. It is a poem that shows his determination to be expansive, humorous, witty, and wise, America's Yankee Horace. He worked hard on it, all that June night, and made good progress. Then at dawn, he set the drudgery aside and wrote "Stopping by Woods on a Snowy Evening" more or less in one go. Dailiness includes night as well as day.

Could it be, then, that writers are most themselves only when writing, lost in work? My guess is that this is so. When I learn a student is taking a creative writing class in order to be forced to write, my mental note is "not a writer, someone who can live without it." And I hear Joyce saying to Heaney, "What you must do must be done on your own."

What is work when we work on poem? What do we talk about when we talk about work on a poem? I once heard the poet Tess Gallagher say that her husband Raymond Carver urged her to write a first draft of a story as if she were on fire. Philip Levine has spoken of his work as being like a coal shoveler in the engine room of an ocean going steamer. Both suggest urgency and labor. What do I mean? A kind of meditation before a blank sheet of lined paper—I do write first drafts by hand—with sporadic scribbling, sometimes of some length. I know when I have been intensely engaged by feeling the impression of my pen on the back of the page. Something I've only discovered later, not something I check on. And as I've suggested, I am suspicious of anyone who says there is romance or glamor in the occupation, except as a regular and ordinary way of creating romance and glamor. Still, it does feel good when you finish and confirm over many days that that poem has amounted to something. It feels good to be released from the very spell you have wanted to entrance you. If writing, writing poetry in my case, has come to define you to yourself, then you will return to it. That is the way *this* writer's work gets done.

When Amy and I lived in a small town in Italy some forty years ago, we would take the bus regularly into Rome to get money from American Express. The bus was a local bus and stopped at many small towns. At each of these towns people got on who were going to Rome, too, but for business of one kind or another. I remember a mechanic who often boarded carrying a bulky piece of equipment, like a brake cylinder or a big spool of wire. Another passenger would be carrying a brief case full of papers and she would greet everyone she recognized. We stopped for coffee and we stopped for a mid-morning meal, a *colazione*. Every time we made the trip we saw many of the same people boarding from little towns and heading into Rome. On our way back, as the day was ending, we often saw them returning. Ten years later we returned with our young daughters to the same small town and were advised, though we had a car, that if we wanted to go into Rome we should take the bus. I'm sure you know what's coming. We boarded the early morning bus and on our route, we saw many of the same people, including the man with the same obstreperous mechanical parts and the friendly woman with the briefcase, boarding. And when we returned in the late afternoon we saw some of these people again. Their routine, which had gone on for years, was moving to us, of course, out of a nostalgia for another time. But in all that time they had apparently been making the same commute into Rome and returning to the same little towns later in the day. I'm not quite sure why I am telling you this story. It could represent habit, a great deadener as Samuel Beckett would say, but for me it also represents the adventure of daily routine. That bus trip from Todi, in Umbria, to Rome, hewing pretty close to the Tiber River all the way, was both the same and different every time we took it. It was pretty much on schedule, but as the seasons changed, it changed, the landscape changed, the passengers changed, except for the regulars. I remember the pleasure a new passenger might express when he saw we were stopping for coffee. We might return as the sun was setting, we might return, as we did on one remarkable late winter evening, to snow and grown men sledding in our little town's piazza where the bus parked.

If I compare the daily work of writing to an adventure, it is only to glamorize it a little, but I also think of it as like a daily devotional discipline, though I wouldn't want to associate it too much with the sacred. It is simply to say that writing is a deliberate practice, along a particular route or routine, which inevitably includes surprises. A set of directed devotions occasionally provides more form than the often wandering notes you have to make when groping your way to a poem. But I also have begun to suspect interviews with writers (perhaps this craft talk is one). If we are writers, what do we want to learn from interviews with other writers? I think we want to know if they write the way we write. Perhaps even how they do it. The only answer to that implicit question that I can give is habitually. Daily. And dailiness is both ordinary and mysterious.

Here is Philip Larkin's "Days":

> What are days for?
> Days are where we live.
> They come, they wake us
> Time and time over.
> They are to be happy in:
> Where can we live but days?
>
> Ah, solving that question
> Brings the priest and the doctor
> In their long coats
> Running over the fields.

Larkin gives a certain metaphysical quality to the quotidian in this poem, which seems almost like an exception in his work except for the telling line, "They are to be happy in," which he must mean ironically. But that long view in a short poem is one you can often find in his poetry. I also like to think that the following poem by Jane Kenyon also expresses the mystery of dailiness. If we know anything about Kenyon's life, we know that simply living an ordinary day was for her an accomplishment. Perhaps you know her poem "Otherwise."

> I got out of bed
> on two strong legs.
> It might have been
> otherwise. I ate
> cereal, sweet
> milk, ripe, flawless
> peach. It might
> have been otherwise.

I took the dog uphill
to the birch wood.
All morning I did
the work I love.

At noon I lay down
with my mate. It might
have been otherwise.
We ate dinner together
at a table with silver
candlesticks. It might
have been otherwise.
I slept in a bed
in a room with paintings
on the walls, and
planned another day
just like this day.
But one day, I know,
it will be otherwise.

Dailiness then is a practice as well as a metaphor, but in Randall Jarrell's poem it is as if water, which is a daily need, were occasionally a revelation, coming almost unbidden from its source, to be itself the source of relief from thirst. Water is a mundane necessity. Its ease of access and arrival from "the bottom of the world" can be seen as miraculous. This happens only after coming daily to the old absurd rusty pump. It means putting yourself to the task daily, putting yourself in the presence daily.

I am not against inspiration. It will come as it comes. I long ago stopped waiting for it. As Philip Levine once noted, the muse does not visit while you're on the court perfecting your backhand. That seems to be one of those remarks to which we might think of exceptions, except that Levine's point is that the tennis court is for playing tennis and the writing desk is for writing. Yet I also remember some twenty years ago at Sewanee that Donald Justice would compose both verse and music on his walks. I remember him sharing a quatrain he'd made up once after coming in about lunchtime. My God it was good. I never saw it in a poem of his, though. Once during the Sewanee Music Festival he returned from a recital with the first two lines of "At the Young Composers' Concert": "The melancholy of these young composers / Impresses me. There will be time for joy." "What do you think of that, Mark?" he asked, as I think I remember. He was worried that though the lines formed a couplet, the couplet didn't rhyme. If you know the poem, you know the brilliant technical but crucial way he resolved that issue.

So let me say again; writing is a personal habit and I would never assign someone a way to do it. But I do think you need to have a way. Still, I find myself in sympathy with the sentiment of the following poem by Adrienne Su:

On Not Writing in Cafés

It's too much like sex in a car:
fine as a concept (everyone needs
to be seen at times by strangers),
but reality seldom agrees.

It's clumsy. Whoever happens
along as you start to forget yourself
is not what you fancied—a relation,
a stranger you know too well.

The hand that isn't holding the pen
flails like an animal pinned by a leg.
And the gorgeous epiphany, just then
at the tip of your tongue, has fled.

I apologize at once to those of you who do your work in Starbucks. It's a personal thing, of course. I simply ask myself to be present in the same regular daily way, at my desk in the study I am lucky enough to have at home. And it is OK if there is no visitation. That easy welling up happens only "sometimes" as Jarrell's poem reminds us. Or as Raymond Carver reminds us in his story "Put Yourself in My Shoes." Myers, a would be novelist, and his wife Paula have introduced themselves to Edgar and Hilda Morgan. Paula explains that her husband is a writer.

"He writes something almost every day," Paula said.
"Is that a fact?" Edgar said. "That's impressive. What did you write today, if I may ask?"
"Nothing," Myers said.

But if Myers's answer were our answer every day, I wonder how long we would persist, and so never reach Muriel Rukeyser's "powerful green hill." Rita Dove's early poem, "Geometry" catches the experience of being in the presence, which may be why poets continue to do what we do. "Geometry" is about the romance of mathematics, but I think the idea applies to writing, too.

I prove a theorem and the house expands:
the windows jerk free to hover near the ceiling,
the ceiling floats away with a sigh.

As the walls clear themselves of everything
but transparency, the scent of carnations
leaves with them. I am out in the open

and above the windows have hinged into butterflies,
sunlight glinting where they've intersected.
They are going to some point true and unproven.

I thought I'd illustrate my own habit of daily writing by taking you through a few drafts of a poem about time and memory and mutability among other things, which is based on a gift of a fossilized leaf from the Eocene epoch that my wife gave to me, after visiting her family in Colorado one summer.

Here is a photograph of the gift and a series of drafts that led to the final version, which appeared in my book *The Heronry*.

Eocene Beech Leaf

Trees owned the earth ~~from pole to pole~~
towering from spring disrobings, autumn
downpours, catastrophes of leaves.
So this singularity, this one ~~
missing an inch of vane along its spine
torn off in the fall or eaten before its descent
is all the more tender for its injury.
Any picture of us now from more than a decade
has this repose and delicacy,
this startling presence of life and death,
preserved as if you'd opened a family book
and the memory lay before your eyes
and the one who placed it there, vanished.
The leaf detached ~~itself~~ from any story
in an album of multifoliate dimensions,
readable on pages of shale like onion skin,
like the young parents, their child, and their unformed futures .
The present turned to ~~dust and shale~~ compressed dust
for 30 million years remembers this clear imprint,
the central spine, the ribs,
fresh as the creator's hand, still palpable,
a ghost filled in with stone for flesh.
What further decay will take the fossil leaf
deeper into its ~~stone~~ vanishing?
A fingertip erodes the sun light
and sun light always exacts an eye for an eye
outstaring the Medusa, outlasting her

Eocene Beech Leaf

Any picture of us now from younger days
has this repose and delicacy,
this startling presence of life and death,
preserved as if we'd opened a family book
and the memory lay before our eyes.
This This leaf in an album of multifoliate dimensions,
readable on pages of shale,
is like *us as* the young parents, *our* their children, *our* their unformed futures.
The present turned to compressed dust
for 30 million years remembers
with a clear imprint the central spine, the ribs,
part of a missing vane, all the more tender
for the injury, still palpable,
a ghost filled in with stone for flesh.
Some further decay may take the fossil leaf
deeper into its ~~stone~~ vanishing.
As for us a fingertip erodes the sun light
on our faces.

Eocene Beech Leaf

printed
This leaf ~~readable~~ on a page of shale
is the present compressed for 30 million years.
Sepia hued ~~The brown imprint~~, clearly green once,
it ~~still~~ reveals the central spine and ribs   *so kept are legible*
but ~~and~~ part of the upper vane missing –
all the more tender for the injury,
a touching ghost filled in with stone for flesh.
It's startling in a way to see so far back
as if we'd found between leaves of a book
a picture of ourselves from much younger days
and remembered everything about it
except when and why we'd placed it there.

Eocene Beech Leaf

This ghost filled in with stone for flesh,
with spine and delicate ribs legible
and a fragment of the fragile blade chipped off,
this leaf imprinted on a page of shale,
all the more tender for its injury,
has held its place for thirty million years.

Startling in a way to see so far back –
as if we'd found between leaves of a book
a picture of ourselves from much younger days
and remembered everything about it
except when and why we'd put it there.

[handwritten annotations:] w/just (The reason ~~for that place~~. we had put it there just why we'd)

Eocene Beech Leaf

This ghost filled in with stone for flesh,
with spine and delicate ribs legible
and a fragment of the fragile blade chipped off,
this leaf imprinted on a page of shale,
all the more tender for its injury,
for thirty million years has held its place.

[handwritten:] fenty

Startling in a way to see so far back –
as if we'd found between leaves of a book
a picture of ourselves from much younger days
and remembered nearly everything about it
except just why we'd put it there.

[handwritten:] fact checker at The Atlantic

[handwritten:] The Heronry

I suppose it's an ekphrastic poem and I know I've written more than my share of these comments on art and objects. And it's also a poem that I began as an exercise, that is, a prompt to myself, just to see what I could come up with about this record of a single leaf's existence and demise and preservation in the Eocene period approximately forty million years ago.

Over a period of several months in the summer and fall of 2014 I lay down a kind of sediment of language about this fossil, excavating, rearranging, paring, and looking for some way to represent not only the thing but its nature as a gift. It was a birthday present from Amy to me, in the 40th year of our marriage. Eventually I arrived at a form—a ghost or relic of a form, the sonnet, which I'd been trying to escape. I had written so many over the years that for a period everything I wrote came out as an octave and a sestet. I even wrote a book of prose poems in an attempt to shake off this paradigm, only to have one critic describe the introductory poem as essentially in sonnet structure. But when I found the form of the poem emerging from the drafts of "Eocene Beech Leaf" I felt gratitude, as if I'd discovered the Platonic script, to use Donald Justice's term, for the poem. There was the available form for what was emerging as the octave/sestet division, though eventually 6 and 5 lines, the tenor/vehicle, the analogy, the dialectic, etc. I wasn't trying to rhyme or write in iambic pentameter. I was trying not to. But I saw that I could link some resemblances of sound and rhythm between the two parts, to convey one of the many feelings the stone leaf aroused in me, the one that through many drafts asserted itself.

Many drafts. I've reproduced only a few that show the more conspicuous changes of the otherwise glacial pace of my revision, my shaping of the material. What am I looking for in the drafts that may, eventually, by a process of daily searching yield a finished poem? I guess it may be the phrases, indicated with arrows, that keep turning up in each new version, until I can see that they will be a permanent member of the thing or will finally need to be set aside, removed, if the poem is going to reach an end, much less a living end. Also I can tell I'm recognizing a form when it begins to emerge, after I cut and rearrange lines and see there is a kind of turn in the movement of the poem.

Was the ending quasi-sonnet the inevitable result? Maybe not, but because I recognized the form that emerged—one that not only seemed analogous but concrete in its representation—I went with it. I took a direction which was both deliberate and arbitrary. Actually I had wanted a more dramatic and word drunk and rhetorical tour de force that would dynamically represent the huge passage of geological time! The final change in the poem was writing, in line six, "forty million years" instead of "thirty million years." When the poem was about to be published in *The Atlantic Monthly*, the poetry editor, David Barber, said an alert fact-checker had reminded him that the Eocene Epoch ended thirty-three million years ago. So, forty million was a more accurate number. Ultimately I recognized what I could have, a poem that was more modest perhaps but which in the end seemed to be the figure in the rock, the dormant shape, the best form for what seems permanent but which is actually provisional, like all material things. As the poet James Galvin wrote in a poem many decades ago, "Matter is a river / That flows through objects. / The world is a current / For carrying death away." Eons created the beech leaf. And eons fixed the fossil likeness of this particular one. And since we are on earth, which as it turns orbits the sun, this process occurred day by day.

I think it is always best to give Emily Dickinson the last word, because from what we know of her life and art, she attended daily on her muse, and I agree with Adrienne Rich that her muse was her own genius. And she recorded her encounters with it in many poems, such as this one numbered 1302 by her latest editor, R. W. Franklin.

The Day She goes
Or Day she stays

Are equally supreme—
Existence has a stated width
Departed, or at Home—

"Existence has a stated width," and that is the space and time we have been given to live, and if we are writers, to write. And each of those days, whether the muse is present or not, going or staying, at home or departing, is supreme.

Writing for God

THE LIFE AND WORK
OF GEORGE HERBERT

T oward the end of his thoughtful new critical biography of
the great seventeenth-century English poet George Herbert,* John Drury considers the literary legacy of Herbert and
the necessity of publication. During Herbert's time, the attitude
of some to prefer to keep their writings from being printed was
considered "the snobbery of manuscript." Herbert's poetry, like
that of his older friend John Donne, did not see publication until
after he died. And Donne left specific instructions concerning
a manuscript of his own—*Biathanatos*, which may have been
a defense of suicide—that when he died, it neither be burned
nor printed. Donne was similarly anxious about the fate of his
secular poems, many of which we know to be erotic. George
Herbert, without Donne's apprehensions about his remaining manuscripts, still kept them private throughout his career.

*John Drury, *Music at Midnight: The Life and Poetry of George Herbert*
(The University of Chicago Press, 2014).

But Drury infers, and I think correctly, that was because "he was writing for God." Fortunately for readers of both Donne and Herbert, publication did come shortly after they died. *The Temple*, the collection that includes most of what we know and value of Herbert's poetry, was published the year of his death in 1633 and went into several printings over the remaining century. Today we might say that Herbert was writing for himself, having chosen a much less public life than some of his Jacobean contemporaries. Reading through *The Temple*, one does have the sense in poem after poem of being in the presence of a private conversation between the poet and his God.

Unlike Donne and Ben Jonson, Herbert was born into the aristocracy. He understood the difference between his rank and the ranks of those below him. He was the seventh child of Lord Richard and Magdalen Herbert. His father died when George was only three and, according to Drury, her husband's death was the making of his mother, Magdalen. She was from an even more prominent family than the Herberts and, after Lord Herbert's death, moved herself and her children into her own family home, there to live with her widowed mother. Drury notes dryly that her family, the Newports, were not only richer than the Herberts but "owned much of Shropshire and were more civilized." Magdalen herself seems highly adaptable and always interested in her children's education. When her mother died, she moved the family again, this time to Oxford, where her oldest son Edward was in school. It is clear that George Herbert grew up in excellent circumstances for a future academic and priest. Whether these were also the best circumstances for a future poet is also answered when we learn that one of Magdalen's close friends was John Donne, twenty years George's senior. Donne was a frequent guest at her table and, when Magdalen died, he preached her funeral at St. Paul's. Her hospitality was so well known that Drury speculates that it could have been one of the sources for Herbert's most famous and possibly greatest poem, "Love (III)," in which the reluctant sinner is invited to Love's table to dine without conditions, but fully accepted as a guest, without the least bit of snobbery:

Love bade me welcome: yet my soul drew back,
    Guilty of dust and sin.
But quick-eyed Love, observing me grow slack
    From my first entrance in,
Drew nearer to me, sweetly questioning,
    If I lacked anything.

Magdalen (this wonderful woman really deserves a biography of her own) never stopped providing for herself and her family. When George was sixteen she married Sir John Danvers, a wealthy man and twenty years her junior and, in fact, not much older than his stepson George. According to Drury, Sir John Danvers married Magdalen "for love of her wit." Her wit was also attractive to John Donne, as well as her good looks, which were equally celebrated. A portrait of her in middle age, included as an illustration in *Music at Midnight*, shows a handsome woman whose face is lit with kindness and intelligence. Donne also enjoyed her connections as he made his way out of his exile as a country lawyer to his eventual elevation as Dean of St. Paul's.

Herbert was fortunate, then, in going to the best schools— Westminster and Cambridge—and being exposed to the best society, and further in having a rich stepfather who was as much an older brother or uncle as he was a stepfather. From an early age his trajectory was toward public prominence. His brother Edward became ambassador to France and his brother Henry, next oldest, became master of the revels at court. Herbert's own studious nature and his tremendous skill at Latin, along with his early ambition to rise like his brothers, led him to become Latin Orator at Cambridge by the time he was 30, a position that some saw as leading inevitably to a state office of the highest kind. It was the job of the Orator not only to oversee

Latin instruction at Cambridge, but also, in the days before the poet laureateship, to provide verses in Latin to celebrate state occasions. But for all this good fortune, Herbert was unfortunate in his health. He seems to have had a long struggle with one of the many diseases collected under the name consumption. His illness may have been linked to his career as a pious student, given often to the mortifications of fasting and abstinence. And then there is another almost intangible misfortune that seems related somehow to his character. He appears to be a man who, having satisfied an ambition, found himself dissatisfied with the position of Orator. It is interesting to note the way in which Herbert's career contrasts with Donne's. Exiled from court for marrying his patron's niece in secret, Donne takes holy orders to climb back into the good graces of King James, and keeps climbing until he reaches the deanship of St. Paul's. Herbert, hardly one to be drawn to Donne's sort of temptation, enjoys the steady rise through the academy that the brightest young Latinist of his day might expect, a pious fulfiller of obligations, writing Latin verses to celebrate a gift to the library from the King or the return of Prince Charles from the continent where he sought a wife. Having arrived at the pinnacle of an academic career, poised for a state appointment, Herbert takes holy orders and serves the rest of his short life in country parishes. Why? Donne's energy and sexuality and ambition are more understandable. But one of the things Drury makes clear is that Herbert's first love was poetry, and taking the humble position of country pastor gave him the exclusive time he sought for his own writing.

Herbert could not have made the choice for the sake of his health. One of his first tasks was to renovate the dilapidated church at his first parish in Leighton Bromswold. Though he had plenty of financial assistance from family and friends in the enterprise, his mother warned him about over-exerting himself. Being a country parson, he learned, was a 24/7 job, and included not only being the spiritual leader of the community, but arbitrator, herbalist and physician, educator, librarian, philanthropist, and host. One of the most valuable services Drury provides in his biography is to reference Herbert's *A Priest to the Temple or, The Country Parson, His Character, and Rule of Holy Life*. This was a manuscript that did not see print until nearly twenty years after Herbert's death. It is a kind of key to the scriptures, if *The Temple*, the collection of poems by which we know Herbert, can be considered the scriptures. Lovers of Herbert usually know the poems in *The Temple* intimately (Elizabeth Bishop surely did), or at least they know the most famous ones: "The Collar," popular for the pun of its title and for its apparent rebellion against the calling of Christ, "Love (III)" (the poem Simone Weil claimed had led her to Christianity), "Prayer (I)," a sonnet in one long dependent clause with an enduring freshness that still seems contemporary, "Redemption," an allegorical sonnet which dramatizes the central precept of Christian faith, and the concrete poem "Easter Wings." For anyone with a sentimental sense of Herbert as a poet available to our modern, post-Christian sensibilities, as Dante and Milton are, then reading *The Country Parson* ought to make them think again. Drury refers to many passages in this remarkable book, whereas Herbert's contemporary biographer Izaak Walton forebears for the sake of space to quote much from it. And yet Drury owes just about every fact he repeats about Herbert's life both to Walton's biography and to his own inference that *The Country Parson* is an autobiographical work, based on Herbert's experience in the several parishes he served. Consider this long, illuminating passage from Chapter 30 of *The Country Parson*, "The Parson's Consideration of Providence," about the pastor's role in catechizing farmers about the will of God:

> The country parson, considering the great aptness country people have to think that all things come by a kind of natural course, and that if they sow and soil their grounds they must have corn; if they keep and fodder well their cattle they must

have milk and calves, labours to reduce them to see God's hand in all things and to believe that things are not set in such an inevitable order, but that God often changeth it according as he sees fit, either for reward or punishment.

The process of thought from this premise leads to some high seventeenth-century logic that might give pause today:

So that if a farmer should depend upon God all the year, and being ready to put hand to sickle shall then secure himself and think all cock-sure, then God sends such weather as lays the corn, and destroys it: or if he depend on God further, even till he imbarn his corn, and then think all sure, God sends a fire, and consumes all that he hath: for that he ought not to break off, but to continue his dependence on God, not only before the corn is inned, but after also; and indeed to depend and fear continually.

That Herbert saw the country pastor's role as one in which he was constantly warning his parish of overweening pride makes sense. But that he was also ready to attribute any disaster that befell the farmers in his flock to the will of God, in fact, to the spite of God when feeling neglected, has to remind his contemporary readers, and the lovers of his poetry, that we are looking at someone whose beliefs may seem jarring and at odds with our own, just as Dante's Ptolemaic universe is at odds with what we know to be the facts.

Though Drury calls this thinking in Herbert "mystical," he does remind us that Herbert's poem "Discipline" reasons with the omnipotent, angry God:

Throw away thy rod:
Though man frailties hath,
    Thou art God:
Throw away thy wrath.

The writer of *The Country Parson* is describing the practical means by which the pastor reminds the flock of its dependency on and necessary fear of the God of judgment. The poet, however, reminds this God with hopeful cajolery that he is also a God of mercy. Poetry draws something from Herbert that transcends the practical application of orthodox belief. Through his own ambivalence and humanity, the poet finds the humanity in God. Here is another reason why, though we may not altogether share Herbert's beliefs, we read his poetry.

Once I reread *The Temple, The Country Parson*, and Izaak Walton's *The Life of Mr. George Herbert*, I wondered which part of the Drury biography we actually needed. In fact, John Drury gives us the needed critical context for Herbert's poetry and he has added his analytical speculation about the relevance of the poems to the life. He also strongly suggests that *The Country Parson* could serve as a key not only to the poems but to the life. Those who would ignore the piety of the poems—and the modern success of the poems is based on our ability to consider their piety, like their verse forms, as a relic—might be made uncomfortable by the practical, class conscious, religiosity of *The Country Parson*, in which so much is assumed about the "slow and thick" (Herbert's description) country parishioners. Granted, Herbert believes the gentry, too, need catechizing, even as they are lighter and quicker on the uptake. He was especially displeased with them when they insisted on entering the Sunday service after the farmers had already taken their places.

I read *The Country Parson* recognizing many of my father's own techniques in acting as a pastor to a congregation mainly of blue and white collar suburbanites. His tendency to join their clubs, take up their hobbies, help them in extremity, visit regularly when they were sick or in distress or needed comforting, loan them money and books from his ample library, makes Herbert's book seem what it is—a practical record and guide. Still, I wonder if a John Donne, installed at St. Paul's, one of the greatest parishes in England, needed to remember how to condescend—and when Herbert recommends the attitude he means it as a form of humility and self-abasement. Again and again, I recognized practices of my father and his father, also a clergyman, in the lists of duties and necessities of the country parson. I don't think we can ignore this dimension of George Herbert's career, even as it seems to be the mirror opposite of John Donne's. Where Herbert forsook the aspiration of a career at court for a life in the country, Donne extricated himself from his country exile and got himself installed in a big urban church. Let me hasten to add, that a big urban church was an ultimate aspiration of both my father and grandfather. They both learned, however, to talk to and deal with men and women with less religious education than they had, though frequently these men and women, their parishioners, were worldlier than either of them. Herbert got his taste of worldliness at Cambridge, as the son of his remarkable mother, and from observing and living among the good country people of his parishes. It is helpful to understand how George Herbert lived and believed in order to appreciate fully the beauty of his poetry. So much of the poetry acknowledges an ordinary human ambivalence with regard to faith. With John Donne, I recognize something else, something more dramatic, especially in his religious poetry—and that is the lineaments of ambition thrown into relief by apprehension and anxiety about the grace of God and the fear both that he may not be worthy of it and that he may not believe in it. I do not mean to imply that Herbert by contrast is more complacent, but he is more aware of the subtlety of belief, especially in its daily practices and encounters with God.

As I have suggested, there are few new facts in *Music at Midnight* which are not either gleaned from *The Country Parson* or included in Izaak Walton's life of Herbert. But halfway through Drury's book, which proceeds from Herbert's childhood, adolescence, and career as a grown man rising ever higher at Cambridge, we come to a chapter entitled "Lost in a Humble Way," and subtitled "Disillusionment." The chapter makes clear that, according to Drury, Herbert felt he had been tricked into the academic life with its worldly entanglements *by* God, without "reflecting on his own frantic efforts to become University Orator." This is not the kind of ironic psychological insight that Walton would even have recognized. Whatever Herbert felt, and Drury's biography includes many subjunctive speculations, 1623 was the watershed year. He stood for parliament, was elected and served briefly, but was not recorded as being an MP in 1624 or at any later date. That year Cambridge also gave him six months leave as Orator. It is known that he was then made a deacon by the Bishop of Lincoln, with the special dispensation of the Archbishop of Canterbury, left his post at Cambridge, and spent the final nine years of his life serving small churches in Huntingdonshire and Cambridgeshire. If, as it appears, the arc of his rise to prominence at court broke off, there is every reason to believe that Herbert himself broke it off. Was he dissatisfied by the life that he perceived ahead? Was he worried about his own health? No one, including his present biographer, knows for sure.

The most curious event in George Herbert's short life, after its abrupt change of direction, was his marriage in 1629 to Jane Danvers, a cousin of his stepfather. Her father, Charles Danvers, had, as Drury notes "a particular fondness for George Herbert," and the marriage itself seems to have been urged on Jane and George by Danvers. It seems to have been little more than the sanctification of a platonic relationship. As a teenager Herbert had told his mother he would dedicate his life to chastity. In a chapter entitled "The Parson's State of Life," in *The Country Parson*, he claims explicitly "virginity is a higher state than matrimony" and therefore, the parson is "rather unmarried than married." This seems to be a Pauline view, but even St. Paul admitted that it was better to marry than to burn. In Herbert's case, though, not being married presented an impediment to his success as a parson. He notes in the same chapter that, for an unmarried country parson, ministering to women alone without an audience can lead to all kinds of rumor and gossip. So, in these circumstances, Herbert concludes, it is probably better for a parson to marry, as long as "the choice of his wife [is] made rather by his ear than by his eye" and that he choose her for "humble and liberal disposition . . . before beauty, riches, or honour." Jane Danvers and George Herbert were married for the final four years of his life. There were no children. The role he expected of her is clearly laid out in *The Country Parson*. Six years after Herbert died, Jane Danvers remarried, had a daughter with her second husband, outlived him, too, and died some fifteen years after Herbert's death. I find it notable that she had a child with her second husband. Though she grieved for her first husband for six years before marrying again, it may have been a welcome change to enter into a conjugal relationship with a willing man.

Besides his writing, the concrete monument which Herbert left was the renovated parish church at Leighton Bromswold. Though no Puritan, he established a plain interior, with oak woodwork by local craftsmen, clear windows, a level floor between pulpit and lectern, and a sense that the congregation itself was on a level with the priest and his associates. Herbert's friend Nicholas Ferrar, made famous by his community at Little Gidding and the esteem of T. S. Eliot, was helpful, especially in the radical design, as was Arthur Woodnoth, Herbert's literary executor, a successful businessman who served as a kind of building contractor. Leighton Bromswold stands today as a model of Anglican parish church architecture. Though it anticipated the Puritan purging of all that was merely decorative, it also subtly reinforced, through its clear windows, a connection between the country congregation and the country from which it arose. Though there are moments in *The Country Parson* that do give me pause, Herbert's sensitivity to the ancient customs of his parishes made him beloved. This was a conventional Anglican priest and highly original poet—they don't need to be contradictory—who was also a good man.

The last valuable aspect of Drury's book is his consideration of Herbert's literary reputation. He explores the Herbert imitators who came along in the decades after the poet's death, often titling their books to echo Herbert's *The Temple*. Most were insignificant, except for Henry Vaughan and Richard Crashaw. He also notes that in the eighteenth century there was a turning away from Herbert's style of poetry—not necessarily from the beliefs expressed, but from what Samuel Johnson disparaged as its metaphysical conceits, its elaborations of metaphor at an intellectual level, and in a kind of Puritan delayed reaction, its apparently overwrought wit and fancy. It is a curious charge, but every century has its blind spots. It was not, apparently, until Coleridge expressed his enthusiasm for Herbert's work that the great poet enjoyed a renewal of interest. And over a hundred years after Coleridge, when T. S. Eliot dismissed Herbert as minor because he was only a devotional poet, independent readers had discovered Herbert for themselves. As is so often the case when critics and poets set themselves up as lawgivers, nothing is more exciting than to prove them wrong. Currently, it is clear that among the seventeenth-century metaphysicals, that is, Donne and Herbert, Herbert is preeminent. I would argue that currently, among all English Renaissance poets, Herbert holds a position of the highest regard. He is loved, as few are besides Shakespeare.

The anecdote that gives Drury the title of his book is one that Walton also relates. Herbert so loved music and the making of music, that he asked to be given his lute on his deathbed and is said to have sung a composition of his own shortly before he died. The apparent ease with which he departed this life is a bit hard to believe, though one thinks of Donne's "as virtuous men pass mildly away" in "A Valediction Forbidding Mourning." Other accounts of those dying of tuberculosis—one thinks of Keats—suggest more of a painful struggle. Nearing his end, Herbert did ask his wife and other grieving family members to leave him, so he could die in peace. The story goes that one night on his way to a gathering of musicians like himself, he stopped to assist a man who was exasperated with his horse that had fallen under its load. After helping the man with his horse and, in a characteristic gesture of kindness, giving him some money, Herbert proceeded to his rehearsal. Known for the care he took with his clothing and his cleanliness and neatness of dress, Herbert arrived soiled and in disarray. Asked about the reason, he shrugged it off and explained what had transpired and said that helping the man as he had—and advising him against beating his horse—would provide a solace for his own conscience that would be "music at midnight" in the future. He also noted that he was not only bound to pray for those in distress, but if possible to practice what he prayed for. So, here is a recognition of the practical nature of reconciliation and atonement. And Herbert provides both in what we know of his life and in his poetry. He knew what it was like to enjoy the best sort of neighborliness and hospitality. He knew how both to accept them and to offer them. He understood the dailiness of faith, as a priest, a poet, and a common believer.

You Are Not Finished

SEAMUS HEANEY'S TRANSLATION
OF THE *AENEID*, BOOK VI

As I begin my review of the late Seamus Heaney's version of the Sixth Book of Virgil's *Aeneid*,* in which the Trojan hero descends to the underworld to visit with his deceased father, Anchises, I am on my way to visit with my still living, but ailing, father who resides in the Northwest. Twice in as many months he has been taken to the hospital for a serious infection. Twice he has recovered and been sent home with antibiotics. He already suffers from diabetes and hypertension, neuropathy in his feet, and has been treated for prostate cancer. He had to give up driving earlier this year. He is 88. His older sister died this year at the age of 93. He was able to travel to her home in Cincinnati, Ohio, where they both grew up, and preside at her memorial service. In his time, as a pastor and minister of the Gospel, my father has conducted many people into the afterlife. And now he has a foot on the threshold, it appears, and I need to see him, since I live so far away.

Aeneid Book VI, trans. Seamus Heaney (Farrar, Straus and Giroux, 2016).

As Book VI of the *Aeneid* begins, Aeneas has lost his helmsman Palinarus, rides his boats ashore at Euboean Cumae, and
seeks the aid of the Sybil who resides nearby. Aeneas has already
reached Italy and his ultimate destination there lies a few stops
up its western coast. The Sibyl's retreat, which is where Dedalus landed after fleeing the labyrinth with his son, bears a relief
designed by Dedalus telling his story but omitting the death
of Icarus because in his great love for his son he was unable to
craft his likeness. The Sybil urges Aeneas to make a sacrifice,
and then to ask about his fate. Speaking through her, Apollo
assures Aeneas that he will achieve his goal of finding land for
his people but only after much bloodshed. When Aeneas asks
to see his deceased father, Anchises, he is given one of the great
tasks of western myth—to acquire a golden bough as a gift for
Proserpina, the queen of the underworld, who will then grant
him permission to enter there. Furthermore, there is news of
the death of another shipmate, Misenus, who must be properly
buried before Aeneas may cross the River Styx. Having built a
pyre for Misenus, Aeneas wonders if his mother Venus might
lend him a hand in finding the golden bough, and lo and behold
a pair of doves, her birds, appears to guide him to the place,
near Avernus. Because he is destined to obtain the bough, he
is able to break it off and return to the funeral rites for Misenus
and even take the time to build him a magnificent tomb. Then
down into the underwold goes Aeneas, led by the Sybil, who
informs him that the ferocious embodiments of Poverty, Hun-
ger, Death, and other monsters they encounter are only phantoms. At the shore of the Acheron, they meet Charon and the
shade of Palinurus, the lost helmsman. Drowned at sea, Palinurus begs Aeneas to help him cross, but the Sibyl rebukes him
(there is a definite waiting period for the unburied dead) and
assures him that he will have a place in history with a temple
erected on a nearby headland that will bear his name. Charon
is reluctant at first to admit a living man like Aeneas to his boat,
because he has done it before for living heroes with ill designs

on the underworld. Persuaded by the Sibyl that Aeneas has no such designs, Charon makes the other occupants of his ferry disembark and takes on Aeneas. Once across the river, Aeneas easily subdues Cerberus, the monstrous three-headed guard dog, with a drugged dumpling. It is by now clear how much Dante appropriated from this book, especially for the *Inferno*. Aeneas spies Dido, exclaims that he did not know she had died, and excuses himself for having had to leave her, but she snubs him and walks off with the shade of her former husband. Then Aeneas comes to the fields of dead and famous warriors, where the Greek heroes cower from him (a very nice touch), and he meets the mutilated Trojan prince Deiphobus, Helen's last husband before Troy was taken. It appears the Greeks, admitted to Troy with Helen's aid, exacted a very nasty revenge on Deiphobus. The Sibyl hurries Aeneas on to a fork in the path and chooses the way to Elysium rather than to Tartarus. But Aeneas is given a glimpse of the fortress of hell on the bank of the Phlegethon. Dante will later describe that fortress and emblazon above its entrance the words, in Italian, "Abandon All Hope Ye Who Enter Here." Aeneas makes his offering of the golden bough, performs some necessary ritual cleansing, and enters Elysium. There the heroes, principally of Troy, cavort and enjoy one another's company while Orpheus sings to them. It is totally a men's club. Here Aeneas meets his father. In a scene almost as poignant as the encounter with Dido, Aeneas three times tries to embrace Anchises and three times discovers that an embrace is impossible, since his father is a ghost. They spend what today would be called quality time as Anchises explains a system of rebirth, which will people the land Aeneas will claim for himself. He identifies the embryo souls of heroes to come, including the whole offspring of the Julians and the soul of Augustus Caesar (Virgil's patron). In a final chilling and clairvoyant moment, he reveals that the ill-fated Marcellus, the great Roman general and adopted son of Augustus, will be the reincarnation of Aeneas himself. With that revelation, the Sibyl and

Aeneas depart the underworld, not through the horn gate, the portal of true dreams, but through the ivory gate, where false dreams emerge. The mystery of this exit has never been solved by scholars.

I asked the poet and translator of Catullus and Ovid, Charles Martin, if he had ever translated Virgil, in particular the *Aeneid*, and he said that he had not; Virgil was too grand. In his preface, Heaney writes that he had to meet "the need for a diction decorous enough for Virgil but not so antique as to sound out of tune with a more contemporary idiom." It is clear that a reproduction of Dryden's stately late seventeenth-century heroic couplets would sound off today, but keeping in mind Charles Martin's reference to grandeur in Virgil, I reread Dryden's version of Book VI and recognized why his translation of the whole epic was the standard until the twentieth century. I also compared modern translations by Rolfe Humphries, Robert Fagles, Robert Fitzgerald, and on the recommendation of Martin, Sarah Ruden. They are variously dynamic, loose, trim, and iambic, but none attempts to be grand, as Dryden is. Decorousness in Heaney's terms seems to be more an attitude of discretion and restraint. Still, there are a couple of passages where Heaney's excellence as a translator can be compared to Dryden's, especially when his elevated diction and deliberate lack of it might be just as effective as Dryden's grandeur. At the mouth of hell, when Aeneas prepares to do battle with the phantoms that guard the entrance and the Sybil prevents him, Dryden translates:

> The chief unsheath'd his shining steel, prepar'd,
> Tho' seiz'd with sudden fear, to force the guard,
> Off'ring his brandish'd weapon at their face;
> Had not the Sibyl stopp'd his eager pace,
> And told him what those empty phantoms were:
> Forms without bodies, and impassive air.

Heaney's translation goes this way:

> Aeneas is thrown into panic, pulls out his sword,
> Swings it round in defence, and had not his guide
> In her wisdom forewarned him
> That these were lives without substance, phantoms,
> Apparitional forms, he would have charged
> And tried to draw blood from shadows.

Not as grand as Dryden's diction, but "tried to draw blood from shadows" is awfully good. And though there are many passages worth comparing between Dryden and Heaney, one more in particular strikes me, since Heaney leaves any sense of the grand or decorous when Deiphobus describes the cause of his death and disfigurement. The Greek heroes, including Ulysses and Helen's former husband Menelaus, have slaughtered Deiphobus in his bed, cutting off his nose and ears. Here's Dryden's version of Deiphobus's complaint:

> Meantime my worthy wife our arms mislaid,
> And from beneath my head my sword convey'd;
> The door unlatch'd, and, with repeated calls,
> Invites her former lord within my walls.
> Thus in her crime her confidence she plac'd,
> And with new treasons would redeem the past.

And here is Heaney's:

>   Meanwhile,
> My paragon of a bride had cleared the house
> Of every weapon and even stolen the sword
> From underneath my head; and now she opened doors
> And called for Menelaus to come in, hoping, no doubt,
> That this grand favour to her lover boy
> Would blot out memories of old betrayals.

Somehow Heaney's "lover boy" as a translation of the Latin "munus amanti" seems tonally more accurate than Dryden's "former lord." As far as Deiphobus is concerned, he and not Menelaus was Helen's proper husband when she betrayed him. His outrage at her treachery and his mutilation, called by Heaney "the love bites she left me in remembrance" and by Dryden "the monuments of Helen's love," is conveyed ironically in both translations. Dryden's "monuments" is a direct translation of Virgil's "monumenta." But "love bites"? Ouch! So much for grandeur or decorum.

Whenever Seamus Heaney set his hand to translation throughout his career, it appeared that he was considering some aspect of his own increasingly public life. Virgil's role as a public poet, the laureate of the Age of Augustus, may have attracted Heaney, although he modestly claims that his translation is more a belated exercise for his high school Latin class. For much of his career Heaney took on (or had thrust upon him) the role of public poet. The English poet and critic Donald Davie in his poem for Heaney, "Summer Lightning," acknowledges Heaney's public profile, especially since the publication of *North* with its brooding Iron Age symbolism of The Troubles. Davie expresses a preference for what he calls Heaney's "early Georgics" and their "pre-Dantesque Homeric virtue." I think Davie must be referring to the poems of Heaney's first two books, *Death of a Naturalist* and *Door into the Dark*, which mainly dealt with rural life (Heaney was a farmer's son), but not without candid historical representations of the problematic relationship between England and Ireland. Davie's reference to Virgil's agrarian poems is an acknowledgment of Heaney's place in an ongoing Classical tradition. Heaney himself at times seemed to struggle with the mantle of this tradition, as it passed to him via Yeats and Joyce. In his introduction to his translation of *Beowulf*, he claims the Anglo-Saxon epic for Celtic and Gaelic culture, and therefore makes it more closely related to Ireland than to England, as if it were Irish culture that maintained deeper roots in antiquity. Other translations and retellings by Heaney have also served as keys to his work. *Sweeney Astray*, his version of *Buile Suibhne*, about the mad king of ancient Ireland, makes Sweeney's flight after the Battle of Mag Rath not unlike the responses of Heaney himself to the obligations of fame and to some extent could be seen as a parable of his move from Northern Ireland to the Republic of Ireland. His versions of Sophocles' *Philoctetes* and *Antigone* grow naturally out of his sense of the poet's role in tribal and internecine conflict. And now the last we shall have from him, this translation of a crucial book in the *Aeneid*, may provide a sense of the poet's awareness of himself in a great chain of Western literature, leading all the way back to the beginning.

In his preface to this translation, Heaney says that in the poem "Route 110," from his 2010 book *Human Chain*, he "plotted incidents from [his] own life against certain well-known episodes in Book VI" of the *Aeneid*. Learning this I have found has made reading "Route 110" all the more moving, simply because the "Mythic method" as Heaney calls it allows for identification of echoes. For example, in "Route 110," the shrine remembered at a friend's house includes oat stalks wrapped in foil which subtly recall the golden bough, and the hurt look of a girl watching the young poet drive away from her house recalls the apparition of Dido looking reproachfully at Aeneas in the underworld. Of course every one of the twelve parts of "Route 110" is meant deliberately to recall parallel scenes in Book VI of the *Aeneid*. It is a bit of a puzzle to identify the correspondences. Is the eleventh section, describing evenings when "we'd just wait and watch / and fish," meant to parallel Aeneas's meeting with his father? Here is the passage that Heaney has translated which describes Aeneas and his father standing together by the Lethe after they have met again:

> Meanwhile, at the far end of a valley, Aeneas saw
> A remote grove, bushy rustling thickets,

And the river Lethe somnolently flowing,
Lapping those peaceful haunts along its banks.
Here a hovering multitude, innumerable
Nations and gathered clans, kept the fields
Humming with life, like bees in meadows
On a clear summer day alighting on pied flowers
And wafting in mazy swarms around white lilies.
Aeneas startled at this unexpected sight
And in his bewilderment asked what was happening,
What was the river drifting past beyond them,
Who were the ones in such a populous throng
Beside it?
      "Spirits," Anchises answered,
"They are spirits destined to live a second life
In the body . . ."

This is so gorgeous I have to make myself stop, but you can tell
how these two poets, Virgil and Heaney, with their agrarian
roots harmonize and resonate together. Here is part eleven of
"Route 110" which seems to have been adapted from this scene:

Those evenings when we'd just wait and watch
And fish. Then the evening the otter's head
Appeared in the flow, or was it only

A surface-ruck and gleam we took for
An otter's head? No doubting, all the same,
The gleam, a turnover warp in the black

Quick water. Or doubting the solid ground
Of the riverbank field, twilit and a-hover
With midge-drifts, as if we had commingled

Among shades and shadows stirring on the brink
And stood there waiting, watching,
Needy and ever needier for translation.

Which comes first, the translation or the need to translate? In Heaney's case it seems clear that knowing the *Aeneid*, in particular Book VI, affected the way he knew this part of his life and the way he translated this part of his life into poetry.

When I reached my father's home in Oregon, I found him in better shape than he had been in years, fitter, happier, and easier to talk to. We had worked for several years on a manuscript of his sermons and meditations on aging, which he had titled *Living the Full Life*. While I was visiting, my stepmother and I helped him put the manuscript into a digital format that he could submit to a publisher online. He and I talked about the kind of cover letter a publisher would want to see and I asked him if he could state the theme or message of the book in a sentence. These sermons and meditations had all been delivered to groups of older Christians, sometimes at church, sometimes in retirement or community centers. Dad said firmly, "You are not finished." That was the message of the book. I thought it played nicely against the sense of completion in the title, *Living the Full Life*. The whole point of living a full life was to consider that it was never complete, never finished. Some time later, while I was finishing this review in fact, I realized that this was the message of Anchises to Aeneas, as he showed him the spirits of the future generations, including his descendants, waiting to be born: *You are not finished*. And then I saw that this was also the message Aeneas implicitly gave to his father by seeking him out as he did. You are not finished, either, not finished being a father.

Becoming and Going

SOUL AND SELF IN FOUR POEMS

Friends of mine in the poetry world have been getting sick and dying. I hate to think it's that time of life. Yet I have been lucky to be around young people who are beginning their writing careers and are full of an excitement like being born. And for some reason coming together in my sense of the world are these two things—friends departing, friends arriving. So I am going to talk about poems of arrival and departure, poems that recognize the moment one comes into being as a kind of birth and also recognize that becoming is inevitably followed by going, hail and farewell, hello and goodbye. Poems of becoming and going. Body meets soul, soul meets body—their life together often takes a particular shape on the page, a form which is frequently narrative, either overtly or covertly. It may be a series of impressions, a catalogue of incremental growth; it may be the story that extends from an extended metaphor; it may be like Dante's, an allegorical journey; and it may be a short lyric that captures a moment and stops time.

These two short poems (which I begin with) possess a clarity that my understanding of arrival and departure lacks. Both have achieved separate kinds of notoriety. The emperor Hadrian is said to be the author of one, his valediction to his soul on his deathbed: "Animula, Vagula, Blandula." It has been translated often, so often that you have your choice of styles, at least from the last four centuries. In other words, a classic, and therefore ripe to be plucked for literary allusion. The other poem I read for the first time in the hothouse library of my adolescence when I made my way through all of the novels of Ian Fleming about his deathless and problematic hero James Bond and came to the haiku "You Only Live Twice," in the novel of the same title.

You only live twice:
Once when you are born
And once when you look death in the face.

Ian Fleming claims that this is "after Bashō," the seventeenth-century Japanese poet, but I have never been able to find the original Bashō that it is supposedly after. Syllabically it is off, with nineteen syllables, nor does it feel right as a haiku. And the novel it is from can justly be accused of salacious oriental-ism. Still, I am interested in these two experiences of what are called birth and death, the experience of birth—and birth can be figurative—and the experience of death, which also may be figurative. James Bond has looked death in the face many times. I'm going to dismiss his implicit boasting and suggest that he and his creator Fleming have come inadvertently perhaps on an actual source of wisdom and delight.

Both poems, Hadrian's valediction and Bond's ersatz haiku, share that connection, umbilicus or membrane, between birth and death and the heightened sense we develop for ourselves along the way from one to the other, if we are lucky. Poets find various forms for this story. It is not a poem of epiphany, but one which recognizes that life has a particular form of mean-ing when we are born (or our sense of self is born) and when we see that we are going to die. Life for the newly born is, as Wil-liam James says, a blooming and buzzing confusion. When with understanding we face the fact of death, life becomes vividly real. Even if, like Prospero every third thought is our grave, we can't live if we spend all our time dwelling on our birth or our death. I think that is why there are not many poems in which the two are considered together as moments of realization. But the kind of poem I am thinking of expresses that amazing sense that soul and body are one, and though they may be severed, a poem is a unique expression of their union.

The emperor Hadrian's farewell to his soul, "Animula, Vagula, Blandula," has not, as Charles Martin wrote to me when I asked him about it, passed its own immortality on to many of its translators. I do think one or two of them has done a creditable job, but I'll get to that. The reason it interests me is first of all, that Hadrian suggests that the soul is not only a bosom friend but an essential part of his personality: his wit, part consciousness, part conscience. And second, Hadrian's poem acknowledges a split which the poems I am talking about also acknowledge, one that ultimately cannot exist if we are fully human. Here is the wonderful Stevie Smith's version of Hadrian's deathbed epigram, in a rhythm that I think must be trochaic tetrameter, like Longfellow's "Hiawatha" and also Philip Larkin's "The Explosion":

Little soul so sleek and smiling
Flesh's friend and guest also
Where departing will you wander
Growing paler now and languid
And not joking as you used to.

We may or may not recognize the author of "Not Waving but Drowning" in this translation. It gives us a clear-eyed sense of valediction to a vital part of oneself, the one that embodies your wit and your sense of humor. Apart from the flesh it occupied, the soul may lose the very qualities that defined it. Without the soul, the body is a dullard. Without the body, the soul goes out like a light.

T. S. Eliot's poem "Animula" alludes to Hadrian's poem in its title.

'Issues from the hand of God, the simple soul'
To a flat world of changing lights and noise,
To light, dark, dry or damp, chilly or warm;
Moving between the legs of tables and of chairs,
Rising or falling, grasping at kisses and toys,
Advancing boldly, sudden to take alarm,
Retreating to the corner of arm and knee,
Eager to be reassured, taking pleasure
In the fragrant brilliance of the Christmas tree,
Pleasure in the wind, the sunlight and the sea;
Studies the sunlit pattern on the floor
And running stags around a silver tray;
Confounds the actual and the fanciful,
Content with playing-cards and kings and queens,
What the fairies do and what the servants say.
The heavy burden of the growing soul
Perplexes and offends more, day by day;
Week by week, offends and perplexes more
With the imperatives of 'is and seems'
And may and may not, desire and control.
The pain of living and the drug of dreams
Curl up the small soul in the window seat
Behind the *Encyclopædia Britannica.*
Issues from the hand of time the simple soul
Irresolute and selfish, misshapen, lame,
Unable to fare forward or retreat,
Fearing the warm reality, the offered good,
Denying the importunity of the blood,
Shadow of its own shadows, spectre in its own gloom,
Leaving disordered papers in a dusty room;
Living first in the silence after the viaticum.

Pray for Guiterriez, avid of speed and power,
For Boudin, blown to pieces,
For this one who made a great fortune,
And that one who went his own way.
Pray for Floret, by the boarhound slain between the yew trees,
Pray for us now and at the hour of our birth.

From Ariel Poems (1929)

I think Eliot wanted us to know Hadrian's poem as we unfolded his deft series of images, his narrative catalogue, with its combination of Pope and Whitman, of the way the soul and the body together come to consciousness. After the title, the poem begins with an allusion to Dante, from the *Purgatorio*. The character Marco Lombardo in the part of Purgatory where the wrathful are purged of their anger gives this beautiful little disquisition, a kind of catechism, here in Eliot's own prose translation:

> From the hands of Him who loves her before she is, there issues like a little child that plays, with weeping and laughter, the simple soul, that knows nothing except that, come from the hands of a glad creator, she turns willingly to everything that delights her. First she tastes the flavor of a trifling good; then is beguiled and pursues it, if neither guide nor check withhold her. Therefore laws were needed as a curb, a ruler was needed, who should at least see afar the tower of the true City.

Dante's phrase is "l'anima semplicetta," "animula" is Hadrian's word. One has to be careful about attributing Marco Lombardo's speech to Dante himself, as with attributing speeches from the plays to Shakespeare. Marco is being punished—actually cleaned or purged—for his anger in this section of Purgatory. What he says about the birth of the childlike soul may not be altogether orthodox. Eliot in his own purgatorial period may have wished to present Marco Lombardo as well-meaning but not yet perfected. Nothing I have found out about Hadrian's poem, extant when Dante wrote, suggests that Dante knew it. This is exclusively Eliot's device. A reference to a witty epigram from a Roman emperor, the poem is launched with a reference to Dante: "Issues from the hand of God the simple soul." With allusions that are a trademark of Eliot's modernism and Christianity, the poem moves through a catalogue of increasingly complex responses to the world, from birth, infancy, childhood, adolescence (a word for growing), and the leap to the understanding of death, and by it, to the recognition of others, their lives, their fates. The world of Eliot's growing soul grows less concrete and more abstract. The last recognizable thing is that volume of the *Encyclopaedia Brittanica* with the small soul curled up behind it in a window seat. It also appears that as the soul becomes a heavy burden, more impaired, less adept, irresolute and selfish, misshapen, lame, halting, it turns abstract at the moment of its own demise and, as if for the first time since it issued into the world, alive. Of course, this is T. S. Eliot, living in the ruins of his first marriage, and trying as much as possible to understand the nature of his own soul and thus every soul. It was a period when he grew increasingly monastic. He wrote some memorable verses at this time, including "Ash Wednesday," "Journey of the Magi," and "Animula." But he also wrote some less good poems for the Ariel series, like "The Cultivation of Christmas Trees" which he described as better doctrine than it was verse. Doctrine seemed preeminent in any case.

I'm not as interested in the doctrine of "Animula," as I am in the narrative of the soul's coming to life and the possibility that the poem starts twice, perhaps three times. The poem advances through three complete sentences, the first 15 lines, then the next 8 lines, and another 8 which end at line 31. The poem's last 6 lines are a kind of envoy and come out of nowhere. The soul experiences a barrage of the senses, given in the poem as a series of parallel statements, a catalogue which in the first 15 lines is quite wonderful. It is a catalogue that could be compared to Jacques' speech on the seven ages of man in *As You*

Like It and the beginning of W. B. Yeats's autobiography. Eliot's lines also bring to mind catalogues in the poems of Alexander Pope and passages from "Song of Myself." The catalogue is meant to suggest simultaneously the appearance of growth and the appearance of living till one's death. The actual images are sparsely distributed, table and chairs, kisses and toys, arm and knee, but "the fragrant brilliance of the Christmas tree" looms from childhood even over the stags on the silver tray and may be matched only by the encyclopedia volume, or at the end of the poem by the disordered papers in a dusty room.

With its 15 lines, then 8 lines and 8 lines, with its occasional rhymes, so occasional you hardly hear them until lines 27–31, the poem may be an exploded sonnet. It argues that we grow more abstract until we die and death makes us a concrete fact again. Life ends at line 31, but the poem makes a wonderful leap to its last six lines, its envoy or sestet, echoing the Ave Maria. Three names are invoked—Guiterriez, Boudin, Floret (continental as the English Eliot might have thought) and two clear fates, Boudin is "blown to pieces" and Floret "slain" by a boarhound like Actaeon between yew trees. Each line reads like an epitaph. And the purpose of the Ave Maria, to petition the Virgin's care at our deaths, is turned into an appeal to her to pray for us now and at the hour of our birth. The creation of simultaneity like that will come back in *Four Quartets*, with the refrain "in my end is my beginning."

"Animula" flirts with rhyme but in no predictable pattern, as it flirts with the form of a sonnet, but more as Matthew Arnold's "Dover Beach" does. We seem to be hearing iambic pentameter, but sometimes we're not. All of the emphasis is on the possible symbolic significance of things and allusions, even at the level of syntax (that Popean chiasmus in lines 17 and 18, "Perplexes and offends more, day by day; / Week by week, offends and perplexes more"). Eliot flirts with rhyme throughout the poem's first 31 lines and iambic pentameter. But he cared for the sonnet as little as he cared for Whitman. Nevertheless, I detect both the sonnet and Whitman in "Animula," particularly Whitman's cataloguing awareness that all things in a list are on the same level. Eliot despite being a monarchist and a Tory has followed a form here in which the soul's sense of the world is of the same value at every step, or rather, the simple or complex is the same soul, issuing from the hand of God or the hand of time.

But what about that? What about that reiteration of line 1 in line 24? The simple soul that issues from the hand of God in line 1 experiences much of the conditioning of childhood as it grows more complicated, perplexing, and grows heavier and seeks escape. But what about the simple soul that issues from the hand of time in line 24? That soul seems to be a stunted one, deformed by Original Sin, incapable of experience, afraid of reality even when warm and good, and dying in a kind of monastic stagnation, living only after the last rites, the viaticum, are administered. I wonder if Eliot is talking about the same soul or even the same creator? We are led incrementally to understand that the soul grows up and can find living painful and seek escape through dreams and reading. That seems familiar and reasonable. Still, it is quite a reversal to bring that section of the poem to an end—at the viaticum for the soul, its final journey—and then leap to the envoy, with its list of names and fates, and finally to the petition to Mary. Or perhaps, keeping Whitman in mind (even, please God, Emily Dickinson), it is a petition to the reader, for we may all be included in the request for prayers. Liturgy here may have more to do with the democratic vista than with courtly hierarchy.

Eliot's own resistance to and horror of experience, "fearing the warm reality" and "denying the importunity of the blood," seem to occur as aspects of that second simple soul, created by time. One of Eliot's biographers dwells on this image of a child curled up alone in a window seat with a volume of *Britannica* and considers it a desolate one. But even Eliot knows, as he shows in poem after poem, that the greater desolation is to refuse what the world offers, though what the world offers leads inevitably to dissatisfaction. I don't think we would care about this poem, if we care about it at all, without its envoy, its last six lines.

Whitman was the great poet of awakening consciousness, and one of the poems of Whitman's I have in mind is "Out of the Cradle Endlessly Rocking." And even if Eliot and Pound dismissed him, we can see his presence here with our own eyes. The best way to chart the growth of the soul is through a catalogue of its experiences from birth to death. When the Virgin is implored to pray for us in the Catholic liturgy, it is now and at the hour of our death. Here aptly it is now and at the hour of our birth. But Guitteriez, Boudin, and Floret are represented only by their names and their fates, the others simply by the directions of their lives. They are not folded into an argument as they would be in a sonnet or laid out in a narrative as they would be in a dramatic poem or an epic. Christopher Ricks reports that Eliot more than once demurred on the meaning of the name Boudin, saying he was surprised to learn that in French the word meant black pudding, a kind of blood sausage, and if he had known he would never have bestowed the name on the friend he was thinking of. I don't buy it. Eliot was fluent in French and behind the name is a grisly fact that it is Boudin's destiny, like a blood sausage, to be blown to pieces. The little soul of wit is not inclined to be nice, which is why Hadrian will miss him. Eliot did have a sense of humor, a wicked one, and as much as he may seem to be depicting his own crippled soul here as representative or universal, he is not above making a sordid joke. His envoy acknowledges others, and their fates, no matter how grim and graphic, but immunizes them, in a way, by asking for the intercessory prayers of the Virgin. "Animula" is one of Eliot's most interesting and complicated poems, because he isn't quite sure of where he is in terms of Christian doctrine (a good thing for poetry). Its narrative provides a way of imagining the countless ways a soul comes to be.

From the high Modernist symbolism of Eliot to the kitchen sink realism of Mona Van Duyn may seem like a disorienting return to sea level from a rarefied atmosphere. And yet we're in the presence of a much more formal organization, but one in which the seams have all been hidden.

The Delivery

I'm five. The petals of my timeless play
can unfurl while Mother hoes out other gardens.
The next-door child and I, alone with my toys,
confine to the dining room our discreet noise.
From the doorway: "*Betty, come here!*" The uprooted flower
falls dead with no warning. What had my friend done,
rolled a dimestore car over the table top,
stood on a chair to wave the little dustmop?
I will never know. She is tethered to Mother's hand
and Mother's voice begins the long scolding.
I start a soldier's march around and around
the table, stomping each foot to stomp out her sound.
Faster around I stomp until it is over,
Betty is gone and Mother takes hold of me,
"What's the *matter* with you? Why is your face so red?
Why, you're *crying*, your whole face is dripping wet!
Well, if that isn't silly, I'd like to know what is!
I wasn't scolding *you*, I was scolding *Betty*."
She laughs. "Go wash your face." The room blears.
My hand wipes and finds all the unfelt tears.

Soon it is supper time. In the kitchen they feed
and talk, while I, invisible as I was
in high-chair days, silently sit on Sears,
wearing the weight of my big and bigger ears.
"Well, you'll never guess what your crazy kid did today—
if that wasn't the limit!" The story swells

into ache in my stomach, then Dad's laughter and hers
slice and tear like knives and forks and a worse
hurt is opening in my middle; in familiar
smells and muddle of voices, mashed potatoes,
dimming light, hamburger, thick creamed corn,
the milk-white chill, a self is being born.
And is swept away through seething clots of minnow
in the nearly hidden creek that weeps through the meadow,
smeared with mud from its suckling roots of willow,
to tributary, to river, deep and slow,
whose sob-like surges quietly lift her and carry
her unjudged freight clear to the mourning sea.
And there they are, all of the heavy others
(even Mother and Father), the floundering, floating or sinking
human herd, whose armstrokes, frail, awry,
frantic, hold up their heads to inhale the sky,
which gilds the tongues of water or soothes them to stillness
with white silk covers strewn with onyx and pearl.
She is with them, inept dog-paddler that she is.
The heavens whirl and drift their weightless riches
through streaky splendors of joy, or bare unending
lodes of blazing or ice-blue clarity.
With them all, all, she is scraped by crusted rock,
wrenched by tides untrue to heart or to clock,
fighting the undertow to shapelessness
in smothering deeps, to what is insufferable.
If those she can reach go under she cannot save them—
how could she save them? Omnipotent dark has seized them.
She can only sink with each one as far as light
can enter, meet drowning eyes and flesh still spangled
with tiny gems from above (a sign of the rare
her watered eyes never need), pointing to where,
up, in the passionate strain, lives everything fair
before she flails back to the loved, the illumined, air.

Mona Van Duyn, from Firefall (1993)

"The Delivery" actually veils its verse form in loose pentameter lines where we might hear a rhyme occasionally. But from what I can tell it is constructed of fifteen quatrains which rhyme ABCC, until the turn at the ninth quatrain in which all four lines rhyme, then the scheme inverts to AABC until the fifteenth and last quatrain in which like the ninth all the lines rhyme. I'm talking about this poem because its extended metaphor of a self being born grows out of the occasion for that birth and offers a form for this story, just as Eliot's catalogue provides one. The care with which Van Duyn has constructed then hidden her effects reminds me of something I heard about Steve Jobs's idea of craftsmanship, that even the insides of his gadgets were to be elegant.

"The Delivery" is the last poem of her final book, *Firefall*. The poem's title refers both to her birth as a poet and to her eventual escape from her family. The poem extends from the memory of an incident in childhood, when a friend she is playing with at home is suddenly and for no apparent reason scolded by her mother. The sense of time and place as the poem begins is almost as ambiguous as it is in "Animula." Yet timelessness is abruptly suspended—uprooted—by the mother's mysterious berating of the friend, Betty. With her command, "'Betty, come here!'" the situation takes on a clarity that makes it all the more memorable. However, the poet has already suggested that she has some sense of her mother's power, for while her mother gardens (if that is what she is literally doing), the children's play is "confin[ed] to the dining room" and their noise is "discreet." She remembers her peculiar response as her mother scolded her friend, marching like a soldier around the dining table, stomping out her mother's voice. When the mother turns her attention on Mona herself, she discovers she's been crying and scolds her for responding to the scolding of the other child. Later, during supper, the mother tells the father, "'Well, you'll never guess what your crazy kid did today— / if that wasn't the limit!'"

I don't think this memory of her parents' behavior could count as a memory of abuse. But the poem does record a psychic wound, and implicitly compares it to a kind of caesarean section which will result in the birth of "a self." It is interesting to note that she doesn't write that the two parents "eat"; rather, they "feed," while the attentive child, "invisible," listens with "the weight of my big and bigger ears." As the mother mocks her sympathy, the poet takes the moment to where a poem of mere grievance might end. There is a reasonable resolution to this remembered insensitive act of parents who were merely being thoughtless, although other poems by Van Duyn give us a sense of their callous self-centeredness with regard to their daughter as well as each other. A "self is being born," but so is the poet, maker of extended metaphors, and all are "swept away through seething clots of minnow." This poem extends past its occasion, changing narrative to metaphor, employing the flow of water that starts with her mysterious tears and, like Alice's tears in Wonderland, forms a freshet that flows to the sea. Van Duyn supplies a form for its figure, beginning in the literal, "the nearly hidden creek that weeps through the meadow," and extending "to tributary, to river, deep and slow . . . clear to the mourning sea." Is that enough? No, for she imagines the humanity that accompanies that newly born self, those whose lives, like Betty's, will move with hers. Nor does Van Duyn depict the poet as heroine, rescuer of the past, recording angel, talented survivor, even though we may infer those roles for her. She, too, is trying to keep her head above water, as she recognizes the terrible and beautiful—the sublime—nature of her progress.

The poet's delivery has been from what was "insufferable." She has escaped a suffocating and soul-killing world, with its formless muddle of food, mashed potatoes, hamburger, thick creamed corn, all in the milk-white chill of the emotionally frigid household. She is fully aware of that escape having begun at that moment in her childhood, when her own simple soul begins its growth, and lifts her and carries her "unjudged freight clear to the mourning sea." She can only go so far with those sinking or dying before she has to flail back to "the loved, the illumined, air."

Weight and weightlessness, shape and shapelessness are as much aspects of the poem's symbolism as they are in "Animula." The difference is that they are part of the extended metaphor's narrative, actions methodically mentioned one following the other, but with the hyper-reality of a dream: the sky "gilds the tongues of water or soothes them to stillness / with white silk covers strewn with onyx and pearl." Above the beauties of the surface, with its sustaining air, "the heavens whirl and drift their weightless riches / through streaky splendors of joy, or bare unending / lodes of blazing or ice-blue clarity." There is a big difference between "milk-white chill" and "blazing or ice-blue clarity" but we can make the connection and see how imagination has created and joined them both. It is the "undertow to shapelessness" that the newborn self has to fight, "in smothering deeps." Others, like the parents, may be sinking there, "seized" by the "omnipotent dark," but she has been there already—she has come from there or a place like it—and will struggle upward, even as an "inept dog-paddler" to the surface of her life and to the air which, for herself and soul, are illumined and fair. As a poem that describes the birth of the poet, "The Delivery" has a rich lineage. What I like about it is that like "Animula" it places us first in an unpromising domestic space, with no mighty forms or gutter nostalgia to elevate it. From a child's seat on a Sears Roebuck catalogue we are launched into a visionary world.

The poet Michelle Boisseau died in November, 2017, two years after being given a diagnosis of cancer which predicted she had only months to live. A number of the poems in her final book, *Among the Gorgons*, show her determination to survive. However, the following poem has more to do with the experience of looking death in the face and seeking a means to describe the experience.

The Obstinate Comedy

In the middle of my life I lost my way.
  I knew my turn was coming, coming
  around the bend. And there it was.
The crows calling over the shoulders
  of trees stretched the space wider
  and wider like the circles a focal
dragonfly sends around itself on a pond,
  but ahead of me something was
  taking up all the space. It was dark
and slippery like things that don't breathe,
  and it was so humongous I couldn't
  see how close it was or get a feel
for its edges. The thing was there
  was no straight way, no mythic down
  and down a spiraling code to climb
up and over a frozen stiff and into a night
  freshly laid with the standard stars.
  My way had turned into a knot polished
smooth as a platitude and I was
  to lie down in front of it, stupid
  and stymied by malignancy.

Standing there with my way knobbled,
  my life (which is all I have to go on)
  seemed odd as a word turned over
and over until it hatches into shatters.
  By turns the tongue in my mouth
  was a frog jinking against my palate
or a wad of soggy pulp. You can't talk
  your way out of this impasse, said the crows.
  You can't hold in the rings of time
said the trees, switching their branches.
  And the knot? Naturally it was mum.
  Obsidian and vitreous, it gleamed

like a symbol while the tumored
  forerunners crabbed my lungs.
  Breathe deep, turn the tides inside you.

In the middle of my life I lost my way
  (or was it more toward the end?)
  and I wandered an abrupt gigantic day.
I saw the trees were upside down
  waterfalls and the crows were flying veins
  of air. Each crow shook its singular crow history,
each tree a history of flying in place, a congress
  of beetles and mushrooms which are
  the fruit of a tree that grows underground.

Michelle Boisseau, from Among the Gorgons (2016)

Like Eliot, Boisseau turns to Dante for a starting point, but with a difference. She appropriates Dante's narrative form as a way to show her bewilderment and fearless humor in facing death, but without Dante's Christian allegory. In Dante's poem, he finds himself in the middle of his life in a dark wood where he diverges from the true path. He spends an entire Easter weekend getting himself back on track, with lots of help from saints and sinners along the way. Boisseau believes she has also lost her way, though not in any theological sense. She knows, as I expect we all know, that her "turn [is] coming, coming round the bend." And her sense is that she has lost the chance to keep going, and now feels as if she were wandering, strangely in place. The chronology of her life has become "an abrupt gigantic day." Unlike Dante, she has encountered no second chance: "In the middle of my life," she writes, "I lost my way (or was it more toward the end?)." The knot of the cancer itself is in the middle of her way, or perhaps it has become the way, since it is a stubborn obstacle which equals her own obstinacy.

My way had turned into a knot polished
  smooth as a platitude and I was

to lie down in front of it, stupid
and stymied by malignancy.

The forward progress of her life is brought to a halt. And the Ptolemaic rings Dante could depend on for his cosmology are, for this poem, "like circles a focal/dragonfly sends around itself on a pond," stretching "wider and wider." Her life is all she has to go on and it has been wound into that knot, and "smooth as a platitude," turned into a kind of cliché before which she is expected to give in. Dante had the undergirding of Medieval Christianity to invest his bewildering trouble with meaning and resolve the dilemma of his comedy. In Boisseau's comedy, she knew her turn was coming, coming around the bend—and "there it was." It's tragic that the expected has come so soon, but the comedy inheres in her obstinacy. What can she do but show a stubbornness to match her dilemma and make a poem about it in which the comedy of allegory is clearly not the point? Eliot might have called this whistling past the graveyard as he does about the speeches of tragic heroes in Shakespeare, trying to cheer themselves up. Boisseau acts to imagine her dilemma not as tragic but with a kind of earthly beauty, "Obsidian and vit-reous," gleaming like "a symbol." She imagines that by trying to breathe deep she can turn the tides inside her. Except those tides are "crabbed" in her lungs and the knot winding her into it is not a symbol, even as an image in a poem. If only it were!

Dante's great allegorical form provides a way to speak of this journey, but Boisseau reminds us that speaking itself is tricky, her tongue, "a wad of soggy pulp" or a frog, "jinking against my palate." Not to be facetious, because I couldn't possibly match Boisseau's gift for facetiousness, even in the face of her own mortality, but her disease is certainly Boisseau's oppor-tunity to display her colloquial invention and her subtle eru-dition, to write as I believe J. D. Salinger once said "with all your stars out." And so that something taking up all the space before her is "so humongous." When she explains, "The thing was there / was no straight way, no mythic down / and down a spiraling code to climb / up and over a frozen stiff and into a night / freshly laid with the standard stars," she alludes to the departure of Dante and Virgil from Hell, up the shaggy, frozen body of Satan, through the center of the earth to the stars at the antipodes. She buries in the allusion to Dante another allusion: the crucial deformation of DNA, the code, which has spiraled into the knot of cancer. Saying there was no way, she keeps her eye on the form she is employing, the tercets of the *Commedia*, and Dante's allegory with its levels of meaning. Would that it were all allegorical—that's the kind of poem she would like to write, but "You can't talk / your way out of this impasse," the crows tell her frankly, and "You can't hold in the rings of time" say the candid trees. Her life, brought to a halt, to a kind of horizontal circling, looks as if it were turned back on itself, so that she turns Dante's narrative form back on itself, too. Hers is a circling that neither descends nor ascends. It is a series of widening circles on a pond which eventually disappear.

In Boisseau's poem the only thing left of the terza rima of Canto I of the *Inferno* is its shadow. As a shadow, it ends raggedly in the last six lines with an inversion of the creation story, and an underground tree of uninviting fruit, beetles and mushrooms. The meaning is all on the surface now. The poet has come to the end of her life when she thought she was in the middle.

Without Dante's poem, we couldn't have Boisseau's, without extended metaphor we couldn't have Van Duyn's poem, without the catalogue, Pope-style or Whitman-style or Baudelaire-style (both Van Duyn and Eliot owe a debt to the French Symbolists), we couldn't have Eliot's poem. These forms grow vitally from their occasions and those occasions have to do with vitality and mortality, life and death, from being born to starting to die. Form is an enduring legacy and each of these poems testifies to its narrative shape.

Recently I shared poems that illustrate the craft of poetry

writing with the graduate poetry workshop at Vanderbilt where I teach. I tried to articulate why they interested me. With the class's help, I recognized that I wanted to talk about a poem which would depict the coming to consciousness of birth or death or both, in an expressive form. At the same time, I wanted to find poems in which there was not too much knowingness, and certainly no heroics on the part of the author, who would be still in the thrall of a dawning realization. In one of our last classes, when we came to the following poem by Sophia Stid and considered and dissected at length to see if the poem would survive, one member of the class said almost sotto voce that I should include this poem. And that is what I am going to do.

Lexical Gap

Before I knew I had a body / did I have one / not
have / there's no verb for what I mean / no word
for this consent-less repetition / we never asked
to be made like this / all clatter / all fragile / ghost
of the heart dimming in and out like headlights
of a car down a long dark curve of road / watching
from a distance we can see how every now and then
everything illuminates / we can't know when or if
it will ever come again / or how / this is my body we say
Sundays but we don't own it / I had a body without
knowing it once / I was a body small enough to sleep
tucked in a plastic laundry basket / I don't mean have
or was / no verb / no word / but here I am / meaning it

This 13-line poem, a sonnet, as I would argue it is, insists on what the other poems have only hinted at. There is no verb and no word (the meaning of the word *verb*) for that moment that you see you are your body and yet know there was an earlier time when you were unconscious of that, though you often have proof, say a story or family picture, that you were once small enough to sleep in a plastic laundry basket (or curl up behind an encyclopedia volume or perch on a Sears Roebuck catalogue or just fit inside your life comfortably). The sonnet form itself, though it may use narrative as part of its argument, tends to stop time, suspend it, in a state of recognition or contemplation. That is certainly what Stid's sonnet does, and without a conventional fourteenth line it manages to create a radiant concentration of images of birth and death, arrival and departure, and the presence of experience, challenging language and the poet's way with words.

Conscience and consciousness may not be synonymous, but they need each other, if anything is going to get said. Consciousness awakes us to life, but conscience connects us with language. Stid shares with Eliot, Van Duyn, Boisseau, and Hadrian the recognition of the dependency of consciousness and conscience. There may be neither verb nor word for their connection, though Boisseau comes up with some choice ones, like *humongous* and *jinking*. The recognition that one has been born is equal to the recognition that one is going to die, and the kind of poem I have been talking about tries to express that equality, the consciousness which is given expression by conscience.

W. H. Auden once wrote, taking his terms from *The Tempest* and the wizard Prospero and his familiar spirit Ariel, that there are Prospero poets and poems, which are occupied with wisdom, and Ariel poets and poems, which take delight for their subjects. I am talking about a kind of poem in which Prospero and Ariel share the same island, as they do in Shakespeare's play, occupy the same haunted space, boundaried by a gigantic day which may be death or may simply be the sense of being alive. Poets always want to find the word for this and sometimes, as in Sophia Stid's poem, that word "meaning" is the only verb. To be is to mean. I know what Archibald MacLeish says in "Ars Poetica," "a poem must not mean / but be" and I hope what I am saying is more inclusive but not all that different. To be is to mean.

Christ, obliquely referenced in Stid's sonnet ("this is my body we say / Sundays but we don't own it"), knew that to be was to mean, before and after you know you have a body. Though it seems obvious that a poem's body is its form, in these poems the form embodies a particular meaning. I know I am guilty of redundancy, since every poem could be said to enact this coming together of body and soul. But it is a particular poem which makes that coming together the occasion for its own existence. The sense that makes such a poem unique and memorable is of being alive even when death is impending, alive at the confluence of arrival and departure.

In memory of Claudia Emerson, Brigit Pegeen Kelly, Michelle Boisseau, Mick Fedullo, Tony Hoagland, and others.

"Something Like That"

A PRONOUN'S LIFE IN POETRY

Webster's definition for the word "something," which it labels a pronoun, an adverb, and an adjective, is "Some indeterminate and unspecified thing." The *OED* adds "material or immaterial." That seems to be often what the word signifies in a poem. Shakespeare loves the word for its full range of possibilities, banal to sublime. Hamlet in particular cherishes it: "Something is rotten in the state of Denmark," he declares and also speaks of the "dread of something after death." I like best the moment when the witches hail Macbeth, in Act IV, Scene 1, of the Scottish Play. They've been mixing up quite a gruesome brew. One of them, sensing Macbeth's presence, cackles, "By the pricking of my thumbs / Something wicked this way comes." And certainly Macbeth has become a kind of inhuman creature by the time he seeks these weird sisters for a final prophecy. His own wickedness has dehumanized him. He appears to be a monster recognizable only to other monsters. And if you consider the stew in the witches' cauldron, with its ghastly range of animal and human parts, Macbeth may be seen as an ingredient, nothing more than a part (tongue of dog, eye of newt), and yet perhaps the thing that completes the recipe and binds the spell. He is the wicked "something" that is coming, the unnamable magic power he contains in his own fate. "Something," then, is not only a pronoun for Shakespeare, but in the case of *Macbeth*, it is an engine of the tragic plot.

Consider next the use of the word "something" in George Herbert's sonnet "Prayer (I)":

Prayer the church's banquet, angel's age,
God's breath in man returning to his birth,
The soul in paraphrase, heart in pilgrimage,
The Christian plummet sounding heav'n and earth;

Engine against th' Almighty, sinner's tow'r,
Reversed thunder, Christ-side-piercing spear,
The six-days world transposing in an hour,
A kind of tune, which all things hear and fear;

Softness, and peace, and joy, and love, and bliss,
Exalted manna, gladness of the best,
Heaven in ordinary, man well drest,
The milky way, the bird of Paradise,

Church-bells beyond the stars heard, the soul's blood,
The land of spices; something understood.

The final epithet or metaphorical name for prayer, "something understood," may be the opposite of what the witches imply by "Something wicked." And yet "Prayer" is constructed as a kind of charm, too—as saying the rosary might be—as various in its parts as the witches' cauldron, and like "the rest" at the bottom of the "glass of blessings" in Herbert's "The Pulley" that something dwells below the other ingredients, like a precipitate or distillation of them, or a support undergirding prayer itself. For Herbert prayer is an act of faith. It may bring us closer to understanding that mysterious something that is God. But more crucially it reveals that God understands that mysterious some-thing which is ourselves.

In both cases—Shakespeare's and Herbert's—the pronoun "something" becomes as meaningful, as charged, as any noun. It is a word with such ambiguous power that it continues to haunt poetry both as a place keeper for a better word and as the perfect word, especially when there is no adequate word for the inexpressible thing, terrifying or transcendent, sublime or ulti-mately consoling. I want to talk about uses of this word and the practical and at times philosophical work it does in a poem.

Love is for poets just as ineffable as it is for any of us. We may be at a loss to describe the attraction of a lover and the aura of desire, but anyone would understand if we said the person we loved had something that drew us or compelled us. George Harrison shows as much in his most famous song, "Some-thing," that it's something in the way she moves, woos, some-thing in her style that attracts him. He can't quite say what it is, but the melody certainly embodies that something and is prob-ably the reason the song was a hit in 1969. Still, I think the over-whelming response to this song, its enduring popularity, has to do not only with the tune, but with the use of that word "some-thing" which stands in for all that cannot be expressed about the lover, the love, the compulsion to love, the entire mystery of erotic desire.

Fate is just as mysterious as love, and certainly as we saw with Macbeth, just as liable to be evoked by the word "something." Again I think it comes of a poet's awareness of how people actu-ally articulate their feelings. Stephen Sondheim's verse for Tony in *West Side Story*, his first song, "Something's Coming," gives us a sense of how the entire dramatic action will unfold:

Could it be? Yes, it could.
Something's coming, something good,
If I can wait!
Something's coming, I don't know what it is,

But it is
Gonna be great!

With a click, with a shock,
Phone'll jingle, door'll knock,
Open the latch!
Something's coming, don't know when, but it's soon;
Catch the moon,
One-handed catch!

Around the corner,
Or whistling down the river,
Come on, deliver
To me!
Will it be? Yes, it will.
Maybe just by holding still,
It'll be there!

Come on, something, come on in, don't be shy,
Meet a guy,
Pull up a chair!
The air is humming,
And something great is coming!
Who knows?
It's only just out of reach,
Down the block, on a beach,
Maybe tonight . . .

"Something's coming I don't know what it is but it is gonna be great." Of course, if you know this song from the musical, then you know Leonard Bernstein's music and you know that the dramatic context pulses with the irony of meeting love, then death—our Romeo Tony's fate. It's one of the most upbeat songs in the American musical theater and, actually, word for word is more carefully crafted than George Harrison's classic. "Something" is personified by the end of the song and asked to come in and pull up a chair. Expected, welcome, still full of potential meaning, with the identity of an angelic visitor, perhaps. We know that Tony is going to meet and fall in love with Maria—she's really something—and encounter and be claimed by Death, that obverse side of "something," "nothing." At the moment he sings the song, though, he is anticipating the future with supreme American optimism. Sondheim's genius as a lyricist is to show what Shakespeare has shown. The word "something" may embody the relationship between character and destiny and the inevitability of fate.

So this mere pronoun if used in the right way can carry the weight of profundity. But I want to turn now to some examples in English and American poetry which show that the word may resonate in a variety of ways, sometimes only to reveal a particular attitude or emphasize a tone of voice, though always with a meaning essential to the poem in which it appears.

In 1955, about the time Sondheim and Bernstein were composing "Something's Coming," across the Atlantic, Philip Larkin's poem "Next, Please," appeared in his second book, *The Less Deceived*. There the resigned pessimism of the English, almost as chipper in its way as American optimism, certainly more certain of certain certainties, pivots nicely on that word "something":

> Always too eager for the future, we
> Pick up bad habits of expectancy.
> Something is always approaching; every day
> Till then we say . . .

But that ship that's coming in for us—the ship Tony hears "whistling down the river"—is, for Larkin, the ship of death:

> a black-
> Sailed unfamiliar, towing at her back

A huge and birdless silence. In her wake
No waters breed or break.

It is interesting how these sentiments about that "something"
that's coming seem to echo back and forth between American and English personalities but are differently inflected. In
American poetry, there is as keen a sense of disappointment as
there is in English poetry—it's just that it usually comes as a
sad retrospect that was not anticipated. Among American poets
Edwin Arlington Robinson shares Larkin's sense of depriva-
tion. "Bewick Finzer," one of Robinson's character studies, has
lost his fortune and with it his spiritual health:

Time was when his half million drew
    The breath of six per cent;
But soon the worm of what-was-not
    Fed hard on his content;
And something crumbled in his brain
    When his half million went.

The American sense of self-worth is often tied to material
worth. Robinson's something is as resonant as Sondheim's, and
both use the word to stand for spiritual wholeness or potential.
For both Larkin and Robinson, the word may have to do with
the relationship between character and fate, but I think there is
a subtle difference, important to both poems. In Larkin's terms,
that "something" which is approaching, death itself, comes for
us all and makes no distinctions about what kind of people we
are. In Robinson's poem, the "something" has to do with how
Finzer has responded to his financial collapse. His collapse
itself was not fated, but it made "something" happen to him psychologically. He is not only broke but broken.

In both Larkin's and Robinson's poems, there is a colloquial
tone to the word "something," which both prepares us for and
surprises us with its deeper implications. It's as if the poet were

saying confidentially to the reader, you know what I mean here. This colloquial, even familiar tone takes me back to Herbert's use of the word and phrase, "something understood" in "Prayer (I)." I know the first time I encountered Herbert's sonnet these final two words stopped me, and I wondered if they actually talked that way about the divine during the English Renaissance. To my ear the phrase sounds contemporary, fresh.

Yet in Herbert's time the word something had a synonym which the King James Authorized Version of the Bible employs: In Revelation 2:4, Christ says to the church at Ephesus, "I have somewhat against thee, because thou hast left thy first love." Subsequent translations have rendered "somewhat" here as "something" or "this," but you can hear at once how odd it would be to say prayer is "somewhat understood," even if it were more correct. My guess is that Herbert uses the less formal word as a way of stepping aside from the Jacobean English authorized for talking about the divine. In doing so, he is able to talk directly to the reader as if he were speaking to one of his parishioners.

I think we like the phrase "something understood." And not only that, but we like something about the way it is said. Wordsworth uses the word to record that very feeling of attraction, liking, in his poem "Stepping Westward." When a stranger on the road greets the poet and his companion with the question, "What, are you stepping westward?," the poet answers "Yea," and sees stepping Westward "as a kind of heavenly destiny." But just as importantly for what I'm talking about, he says:

> I liked the greeting; 'twas a sound
> Of something without place or bound;
> And seemed to give me spiritual right
> To travel through that region bright.

In this case, the word implies a destination of limitless potential as well as the poet's gratitude to have that feeling instilled in him by a stranger's passing comment.

Several modern and contemporary American poets are notable for their use of the word "something," always colloquially, to convey, as Wordsworth and Herbert have done, complicated feelings for which more complicated language will not do. Robert Frost has an especial fondness for the word and uses it with great variety, but most often as a sign of the transcendent, or when the language of transcendence—fate, divinity, the immanent will—has been exhausted. Frost turns to the word in a number of other ways, too. "Something there is that doesn't love a wall," he begins "Mending Wall," the first poem in *North of Boston*. The word appears to stand in for the workings of nature. He also suggests that "something" could be "Elves," or some other supernatural force. And later, in *North of Boston*, he deploys it differently once more in the exchange between Mary and Warren about Silas, the hapless and undependable hired man, in "The Death of the Hired Man." Mary tells her husband that Silas "has come home to die" and what follows is an exchange about the meaning of home. Warren says:

> Home is the place where, when you have to go there,
>   They have to take you in.

And Mary almost as if groping for words responds:

> I should have called it
> Something you somehow haven't to deserve.

It's Warren's phrase that we may remember from this poem. But it is Mary's that I find most moving. Unwittingly, she comes close to defining Grace—which is always undeserved—as the natural gift of being accepted back home.

Frost uses "something" so often and so meaningfully that it would be possible only to refer to him in this essay. And he as often attaches a dark as a bright connotation to the word. Take the Witch of Coös, in Frost's poem of the same name, relating her psychic powers and their limitations:

Tell you what Ralle the Sioux Control once told me.
He said the dead had souls, but when I asked him
How could that be—I thought the dead were souls,
He broke my trance. Don't that make you suspicious
That there's something the dead are keeping back?
Yes, there's something the dead are keeping back.

Here through the Witch's weird sense of the afterlife, Frost manages to express with just two uses of the word "something," the darker implications of spiritualism, a pseudo-science that was rampant at the time he wrote the poem. And of course if you know the poem, you know that it's the Witch herself who is holding something back—the murder of her lover whom she and her husband stashed many years before in their cellar. Frost also knows when "something" is the right wrong word. When the young couple in his great poem "Home Burial" are arguing about the meaning of their child's death, the husband implores his wife to share her grief with him. First he makes a reasonable appeal. He says, "Don't carry it to someone else this time." Then he adds, "Tell me about it if it's something human." He uses exactly the right word, "something," to say exactly the wrong thing.

Perhaps the poem that best exemplifies Frost's usage of the word is "For Once, Then, Something." A poem from *New Hampshire*, it is in fifteen lines of hendecasyllables, eleven-syllable lines, falling and rising and falling again, but without rhyme, perhaps an exercise in a Classical meter:

Others taunt me with having knelt at well-curbs
Always wrong to the light, so never seeing
Deeper down in the well than where the water
Gives me back in a shining surface picture
Me myself in the summer heaven godlike
Looking out of a wreath of fern and cloud puffs.

Once, when trying with chin against a well-curb,
I discerned, as I thought, beyond the picture,
Through the picture, a something white, uncertain,
Something more of the depths—and then I lost it.
Water came to rebuke the too clear water.
One drop fell from a fern, and lo, a ripple
Shook whatever it was lay there at bottom,
Blurred it, blotted it out. What was that whiteness?
Truth? A pebble of quartz? For once, then, something.

The final phrase, anticipated in the title, is justly famous. But it is
also the whiteness of that "something" which gives the word its
mystery. That "something white, uncertain" is also "Something
more of the depths." (Emily Dickinson and Herman Melville
both knew the sublimity and terror of that color.) Here I think
we are as much looking into the depths of the witches' cauldron as we are looking heavenward in Herbert's "Prayer," because whatever that "something" was in Frost's poem—"Truth?
A pebble of quartz?"—still, "something" is there. Abstract or
concrete, good or evil, it is not nothing, and for Frost, that's as
much a statement of faith as Herbert's "something understood."

Of course, "nothing" is the opposite of "something," and some
would prefer the antonym in representing or refusing to speak
of ineffable things, transcendent things. Frost's great counter-
weight here is Wallace Stevens, whose Snow Man as "nothing
himself, beholds / Nothing that is not there, and the nothing
that is." I could go back and forth between "nothing" and "something" with these two old wizards, but instead I am going to talk
about Elizabeth Bishop, who employed the word "something"
as Frost and Herbert did, while sharing Stevens's doubts about
faith and its representation in language.

Bishop's love of George Herbert's poetry does not preclude
the skepticism of religious belief she shares with Wallace Stevens. Both may be echoed in her poem "Seascape" from her first
book, *North & South,* in 1946.

This celestial seascape, with white herons got up as angels,
flying high as they want and as far as they want sidewise
in tiers and tiers of immaculate reflections;
the whole region, from the highest heron
down to the weightless mangrove island
with bright green leaves edged neatly with bird-droppings
like illumination in silver,
and down to the suggestively Gothic arches of the mangrove
    roots
and the beautiful pea-green back-pasture
where occasionally a fish jumps, like a wildflower
in an ornamental spray of spray;
this cartoon by Raphael for a tapestry for a Pope:
it does look like heaven.
But a skeletal lighthouse standing there
in black and white clerical dress,
who lives on his nerves, thinks he knows better.
He thinks that hell rages below his iron feet,
that that is why the shallow water is so warm,
and he knows that heaven is not like this.
Heaven is not like flying or swimming,
but has something to do with blackness and a strong glare
and when it gets dark he will remember something
strongly worded to say on the subject.

I have no way of knowing for sure, but I like to think that the
"skeletal lighthouse" depicted in "black and white clerical dress"
is meant to recall Father Herbert. John Drury's recent biography of Herbert, *Music at Midnight*, reminds us that he was tall,
ascetically thin, pious, and yet with a love of music and a taste
for nice clothes. Perhaps Herbert and his like are on Bishop's
mind with genuine though satirical affection. The image of the
beam from the lighthouse as a form of speech is brilliant. And
the word "something," as if it were a bracing and oracular passage of scripture—John 1:5 comes to mind, "And the light shi-

neth in darkness; and the darkness comprehended it not," but also Psalm 36:9, "in thy light shall we see light"—is fairly blinding in its implication: the priestly lighthouse may not have the scripture on its tongue now, in the lovely daylight scene depicted, but once he's in his element—darkness—he'll think of it and broadcast its message.

There are times when the word's serviceability as a placeholder becomes apparent, that is, when the word "something" doesn't seem to mean anything besides itself and could be waiting for a better word to replace it. Bishop's mastery is to show us both the limitation of meaning while at the same time the precision of observation that can be represented by the pronoun, so that we realize that there is not another word that will do. Here, from Bishop's third book, *Questions of Travel*, from the second section, "Elsewhere," is the poem "Sandpiper."

The roaring alongside he takes for granted,
and that every so often the world is bound to shake.
He runs, he runs to the south, finical, awkward,
in a state of controlled panic, a student of Blake.

The beach hisses like fat. On his left, a sheet
of interrupting water comes and goes
and glazes over his dark and brittle feet.
He runs, he runs straight through it, watching his toes.

— Watching, rather, the spaces of sand between them
where (no detail too small) the Atlantic drains
rapidly backwards and downwards. As he runs,
he stares at the dragging grains.

The world is a mist. And then the world is
minute and vast and clear. The tide
is higher or lower. He couldn't tell you which.
His beak is focussed; he is preoccupied,

looking for something, something, something.
Poor bird, he is obsessed!
The millions of grains are black, white, tan, and gray,
mixed with quartz grains, rose and amethyst.

If you've listened to the composer Elliott Carter's setting of this poem, from his sequence of Bishop settings, "A Mirror on Which to Dwell," you've heard the "controlled panic" in the phrase, "looking for something, something, something." In "Sandpiper" it is not so much the word itself that conveys meaning—the bird is simply looking for food—but its repetition. To a human being the bird's hunting might look like anxiety or, as the poem implies, obsession. It is possible to read the poem as a reflection of the poet's own pursuit of poetry, her obsessive searching for words in a world that is "minute and vast and clear"; however, for the animal it is a necessary activity and not self-conscious or neurotic. Though Bishop calls the bird a student of Blake, possibly looking to see "a World in a Grain of Sand," as Blake writes in "Auguries of Innocence," she shows herself to be a keen student of nature. It is the phenomenon of the bird's act of self-preservation she records in writing "looking for something, something, something," as well as its objectification as a figure of speech or symbol for the poet or artist.

The desire to make the word "something" mean something can be related to the tendency of language, including the language of poetry, to turn its subjects into objects, limited to the purposes of representation, and as a paradoxical result diminished in their own reality, even as they may be enhanced. When the witch senses the approach of Macbeth as "Something wicked," she has done exactly that, taken the reality of his humanity and turned him into an "it," but to great poetic and dramatic effect. The word "something" has the power to objectify and, in the hands of certain poets, may be used for its critical and political implications, especially when it comes to race.

In her poem "The Lovers of the Poor," Gwendolyn Brooks employs the satiric value of the word as she depicts the ladies from the Ladies' Betterment League in a slum dwelling in Chicago, come to dispense money to the worthy poor, and encountering the stench of "urine, cabbage, and dead beans . . . and, they're told, / *Something* called chitterlings." However, she teaches us its murkier and more sinister implications in her poem about the Emmett Till murder, "A Bronzeville Mother Loiters in Mississippi. Meanwhile, a Mississippi Mother Burns Bacon." In this poem she depicts Carolyn Bryant, Emmett Till's accuser, whose husband took part in the boy's lynching. She is making breakfast for her husband and trying to imagine that he has saved her, a maiden in distress, like some noble hero in a ballad who has vanquished a brutal knave, even though the latter is a fourteen-year-old black boy.

> It occurred to her that there may have been something
> Ridiculous in the picture of the Fine Prince
> Rushing (rich with the breadth and height and
> Mature solidness whose lack, in the Dark Villain, was
>   impressing her,
> Confronting her more and more as this first day after the trial
> And acquittal wore on) rushing
> With his heavy companion to hack down (unhorsed)
> That little foe.

Yes, it is "something / Ridiculous," but a something freighted with ignorance and hatred. In imagining the other as fictional, as Carolyn Bryant is trying to do to justify her accusation of Emmett Till, the word "something" can stand in for what is actually a failure of imagination, and the results are evil. Something wicked this way comes indeed.

Garrett Hongo, in his poem "Four Chinatown Figures," also employs "something" for its objectifying power. In his poem a couple of young white urban professionals, out on a date, linger near the wishing well in L.A.'s Chinatown, and bump into two Chinese dishwashers on a cigarette break. The man at first feels threatened but then dismisses them, yet the woman sees them in "suspense/thriller prose," and it is from her point of view that "Something grins on the face of the taller, fairer-complected one, / glints from his foxteeth, smolders in breathfog, camphor about to flare." She urges her date to turn away with her, so misses the "fair one" saying, *Kiss me, white ghost.*" The word "something" here gives us that objectifying gaze, that fiction of the other, projected from one character and then back from another. The poet himself is part of a triangulation, and that word "something" includes him as the one who imagined the scene.

To objectify a subject, especially with the apparent ambiguity of the word "something," can also result in a study of the act. Clearly in Brooks's and Hongo's poems the act is racism. But what is it in Robert Creeley's "Something"? Is it a critique of the male gaze? It looks as if it may be, but I'm not so sure.

> I approach with such
> a careful tremor, always
> I feel the finally foolish
>
> question of how it is,
> then, supposed to be felt,
> and by whom. I remember
>
> once in a rented room on
> 27th street, the woman I loved
> then, literally, after we
>
> had made love on the large
> bed sitting across from
> a basin with two faucets, she
>
> had to pee but was nervous,
> embarrassed I suppose I
> would watch her who had but

a moment ago been completely
open to me, naked, on
the same bed. Squatting, her

head reflected in the mirror,
the hair dark there, the
full of her face, the shoulders,

sat spread-legged, turned on
one faucet and shyly pissed. What
love might learn from such a sight.

How are we to take this, a poem from the mid-twentieth century, with our greater political consciousness of how we por-
tray one another, how we may diminish or exploit one another,
through representation? Here I think the title of the poem,
"Something," does not finally refer to the woman as an object
in the poem—it may seem that way, yes, but I don't think it
does. It refers to "What / love might learn from such a sight."
In some cases not only will this evocative pronoun be required,
but tautology, also, is the only way of speaking, a redundancy
which is in fact revelatory. Remember *Webster*'s definition for
the pronoun "something": "Some indeterminate and unspecified thing." Remove the two adjectives before "thing" and you
have the essential tautology of the word itself, i.e. "something"
is "some thing." Robert Frost, a great lover of tautology, shows
its efficacy when, at the end of "Hyla Brook," he states, "We
love the things we love for what they are." Creeley has come
to a similar understanding, and two pronouns, "something"
and its kin "what" have helped him to express that understanding. "Something" in his poem is "What / love might learn." Intimacy makes the body of the beloved actual, not a fiction. It
could be that in this poem our young poet records something
that is crucial to loving, the sight of his lover's body at a moment
of poignant vulnerability.

I want to end with the poem "First Thought" by Brenda Hillman. This poem collects many of my observations about the effects of the word "something," in particular when it is used most consciously *as* a word, a provisional word, even a place-holder, tentative, unstable, yet charged with such inexpressibility that it can be compared only to another pronoun, as it is in the poem's last line, which is the title of this essay.

The first thought
was rage—

In certain systems, the point at which that thought
emerges from God's mind is his consort,
but before she turns her rage onto the world, the violent
lords must give her the body of a woman which is not easy.
Imagine them standing around before they will trap
God's vague thought into female flesh. The way
their robes undulate, the slightly yellowing raiment—

poor things.
They will not understand the rage.
It will be expressed forever in the split in things.
In the two-toned lupine,
in the cupped, silk lining of the tulip,
in the red and white of all armies in all wars,
it will bend over my dream wearing his face.

The moment my daughter was lifted
from me, that sticky
flesh screamed fury,
for she, too, blamed the female body—
I loved it that she screamed—

and I knew I had been sent to earth to understand that pain.

The nurses moved about, doing something
over to the left. Probably weighing her

on what looked like blue tin. The flash of non-
existence always at the edge of vision,
and in the next moment, some unasked-for radiance.

Under those lights,
the nurses seemed shabby—
the ivory lords, come haltingly
into the bridal chamber, slightly yellowing raiment.

The last pain on earth will not be the central pain,
it will be the pain of the soul and not the body,
the pain of the body will be long since gone,
absorbed into the earth, which made it beautiful—

don't you love the word raiment?
Dawn comes in white raiment.
Something like that

I do not know enough about the kind of Gnosticism behind
this poem. Much of the book *Bright Existence*, in which it is
included, investigates the journey of the individual soul into
this world, but I do know a particular mysticism is suggested,
one in which, as this poem shows, birth itself is a kind of wedding, even a reluctant one, between the mind of God and the
physical world. The poet describes the birth of her daughter in
these terms. The poem introduces two words, "raiment" and
"something," before its conclusion in which both will become
resonant. Moving from images of the mythical embodiment of
the female in a vague thought of God, an embodiment which
is represented in all kinds of dualities, to the literal drama of
the delivery room, in which the nurses seem poor representations of mythic figures ("shabby" rather than lordly) attending
this wedding, the poet embarks on a brief expression of what?
The eschatology of what she calls this "system"? How the pain
which the soul undergoes in becoming a body will be the last
but not the central pain on earth? I have to admit that I get a

little lost here. But as if sensing the reader's possible confusion, the poet changes the subject, transforming the end—the last pain on earth—to a beginning, dawn, as in the beginning of a human life. As if distracted, she follows this wonderful tangent into the physical beauty of a word in itself. She finds the way of speaking she wants ("don't you love the word raiment"), the image she wants ("Dawn comes in white raiment"), and the way she wants to express its meaning ("Something like that").

Whatever "something" is and whatever "that" is, at this moment they are like each other. They evoke and call each other forth. They somehow mean each other. The phrase is condensed, like the image it refers to—"Dawn comes in white raiment"—and even takes on the physical properties Ezra Pound hoped for in the ideogram. And "Something like that" is colloquial, like Herbert's "something understood." It is redundant and revelatory, understated and epiphanic, an apparent falling short which also lands perfectly, an expression of the inexpressible, done with offhanded grace as if there were nothing to it. There's no other way to respond except through affirmation. Yes, raiment is a word to love. Yes, dawn could be said to come in white raiment. Yes, the birth of this child certainly is something like that. Yes, Robert Frost was right: we do love the things we love for what they are, like the body of our lover or our newborn baby. And we hope that we are loved for what we are, that unique something that constitutes our individuality, and understood, too.

Acknowledgments

Some of the essays in this book have been previously published in different form:

"When the Light Came On: The Epic *Gilgamesh*," *The Hudson Review*, vol. 58, no. 2 (summer 2005). A review of *Gilgamesh: A New English Version*, trans. Stephen Mitchell.

"To Make the Final Unity: Metaphor's Matter and Spirit," *The Southern Review*, vol. 43, no. 2 (spring 2007).

"The Story of a Feeling: Poetry's Passionate Repetition," *The Writer's Chronicle*, vol. 39, no. 2 (October/November 2006).

"American Devotions," *Blackbird*, vol. 11, no. 1 (June 2012). http://www.blackbird.vcu.edu/v11n1/nonfiction/jarman_m/devotions_page.shtml

"Writing for God: The Life and Work of George Herbert," *The Hudson Review*, vol. 67, no. 2 (summer 2014). A review of *Music at Midnight: The Life & Poetry of George Herbert* by John Drury.

"You Are Not Finished: Seamus Heaney's Translation of the *Aeneid* Book VI," *The Hudson Review*, vol. 69, no. 3 (autumn 2016).

"'Something like That': A Pronoun's Life in Poetry," *The Sewanee Review*, vol. 125, no. 3 (summer 2017).

The author and publisher gratefully acknowledge the following
additional sources:

John Berryman, "Eleven Addresses to the Lord" from *Collected
Poems 1937–1971*. Copyright © 1989 by Kate Donahue Berryman. Reprinted by permission of Farrar, Straus & Giroux, LLC.

Elizabeth Bishop, "Seascape" and "Sandpiper" from *The Complete
Poems 1927–1979*. Copyright © 2011 by The Alice Helen Meth-
fessel Trust. Reprinted by permission of Farrar, Straus & Giroux, LLC.

Michelle Boisseau, "Time Done Is Dark–Archibald MacLeish"
from *A Sunday in God-Years*. Copyright © 2009 by Michelle
Boisseau. Reprinted with the permission of The Permissions
Company, Inc., on behalf of the University of Arkansas Press.
"The Obstinate Comedy" from *Among the Gorgons*. Copyright © 2016 by Michelle Boisseau. Reprinted with the permission of the University of Tampa Press.

Robert Creeley, "Something" from *The Collected Poems of Robert
Creeley*. Copyright © 1967 by Robert Creeley. Reprinted by
permission of the University of California Press.

Kate Daniels, "Farewell to the Maiden" from *Four Testimonies*
(Baton Rouge: LSU Press, 1998). Copyright © 1998 by Kate
Daniels. Reprinted with the permission of the author.

Emily Dickinson, 1551 ["Those—dying then"] and 1302 ["The
Day She goes"] from *The Poems of Emily Dickinson*, edited by
Thomas H. Johnson Cambridge, Mass.: The Belknap Press of
Harvard University Press. Copyright 1951, © 1955 by the President and Fellows of Harvard College. Copyright © renewed
1979, 1983 by the President and Fellows of Harvard College.
Copyright 1914, 1918, 1919, 1924, 1929, 1930, 1932, 1935, 1937,
1942, by Martha Dickinson Bianchi. Copyright 1952, © 1957,
1958, 1963, 1965, by Mary L. Hampson.

Rita Dove, "Geometry" from *The Yellow House on the Corner*,
Carnegie Mellon University Press, Pittsburgh, PA. © 1980 by
Rita Dove. Reprinted by permission of the author.

T. S. Eliot, "Animula" from *Collected Poems: 1909–1962*. Copyright 1929, renewed © 1964 by T. S. Eliot. Reprinted by permission of Houghton Mifflin Harcourt Publishing Company. All rights reserved.

Ian Fleming, haiku from *You Only Live Twice* (London: Jonathan Cape, 1964). Copyright © 1964 by Ian Fleming Publications, Ltd. Reprinted with the permission of Ian Fleming Publications Ltd.

Robert Frost, "I Could Give All to Time" and "For Once, Then, Something" from *The Poetry of Robert Frost*, edited by Edward Connery Lathem. Copyright © 1969 by Henry Holt and Company, Inc. Reprinted by permission of Henry Holt and Company, LLC.

Seamus Heaney, excerpt from "Route 110" from *Human Chain*. Copyright © 2010 by Seamus Heaney. Reprinted by permission of Farrar, Straus & Giroux, LLC and Faber and Faber, Ltd.

Brenda Hillman, "First Thought" from *Bright Existence*. Copyright © 1993 by Brenda Hillman. Reprinted by permission of Wesleyan University Press.

Andrew Hudgins, "Beatitudes" from *Ecstatic in the Poison*. Copyright © 2003 by Andrew Hudgins. Reprinted with the permission of The Overlook Press.

Mark Jarman, Unholy Sonnets 9 ["Almighty God, to you all hearts are open"], 11 ["Half asleep in prayer I said the right thing"]; and 14 ["After the praying, after the hymn singing"], "To a Brainy Child in Distress," and "The Prayer Chain" from *Bone Fires: New and Selected Poems*. Copyright © 1997, 2011 by Mark Jarman. "Eocene Beech Leaf" from *The Heronry*. Copyright © 2017 by Mark Jarman. All reprinted with the permission of The Permissions Company, LLC on behalf of Sarabande Books, www.sarabandebooks.org.

Randall Jarrell, "Well Water" from *The Complete Poems*. Copyright © 1969 by Randall Jarrell, renewed 1997 by Mary von S. Jarrell. Reprinted by permission of Farrar, Straus & Giroux, LLC.

Sophia Stid, "Lexical Gap." Reprinted by permission of the author.

Adrienne Su, "On Not Writing in Cafés" from *Having None of It*. Copyright © 2009 by Adrienne Su. Reprinted with the permission of Manic D Press.

Chase Twichell, "The Myths" from *Dog Language*. Copyright © 2005 by Chase Twichell. "Aisle of Dogs" from *Horses Where the Answers Should Have Been: New and Selected Poems*. Copyright © 1995 by Chase Twichell. Both reprinted with the permission of The Permissions Company LLC on behalf of Copper Canyon Press, www.coppercanyonpress.org.

Jean Valentine, excerpts from *Lucy: A Poem*. Copyright © 2009 by Jean Valentine. Reprinted with the permission of The Permissions Company LLC on behalf of Sarabande Books, Inc., www.sarabandebooks.org.

Mona Van Duyn, "The Delivery" from *Firefall*. Copyright © 1993 by Mona Van Duyn. Used by permission of Alfred A. Knopf, an imprint of the Knopf Doubleday Publishing Group, a division of Penguin Random House LLC. All rights reserved.

Virgil, excerpts from *Aeneid Book VI: A New Verse Translation, Bilingual Edition*, translated by Seamus Heaney. Copyright © 2016 by Seamus Heaney. Reprinted by permission of Farrar, Straus & Giroux, LLC and Faber & Faber, Ltd.

CPSIA information can be obtained
at www.ICGtesting.com
Printed in the USA
JSHW021447121219
2926JS00003B/6